"This wonderful book is as moving and inspiring as its story is poignant and powerful. One simply must believe in a sense of Divine Choreography reading how these incredible three brothers were led to the loving arms of their dads. John Sonego is so self-disclosing and disarmingly vulnerable in telling all their stories that I was frequently moved to tears. In the process he reveals what truly great parenting these lucky boys are receiving."

*--- Judith Light, Actor*

"This book should be required reading for every parent. John and Michael's story of adopting three brothers and creating a loving and caring family is magnificent. While not intended as instructions for parents, John's beautifully written anecdotes provide us with real-life parenting models to ensure that our kids will be healthy and happy right now and will grow up to be strong, productive, and loving adults. The fact that John and Michael are gay is secondary to the more important theme about responsible, loving and successful parenting."

*--Hal Zina Bennett, parent, grandparent, and*
*author of Write From the Heart:*
*Unleashing the Power of Your Creativity*

D1563045

# My Three Sons
## The Birth of a New Family (A True Story)

John Sonego

iUniverse, Inc.
New York   Bloomington

**My Three Sons**
**The Birth of a New Family**

*iUniverse books may be ordered through booksellers or by contacting:*

*iUniverse*
*1663 Liberty Drive*
*Bloomington, IN 47403*
*www.iuniverse.com*
*1-800-Authors (1-800-288-4677)*

*Because of the dynamic nature of the Internet, any Web addresses or links contained in this book may have changed since publication and may no longer be valid.*

*ISBN: 978-1-4401-3418-0 (pbk)*
*ISBN: 978-1-4401-3420-3 (cloth)*
*ISBN: 978-1-4401-3419-7 (ebk)*

*Printed in the United States of America*

*iUniverse rev. date: 4/21/2009*

*For Sherman.*
Who shares with her children
an unerring insight
that comes from lifetimes on this earth.
I love you.

*And*

*for Michael*
who was glad to walk this
journey together

*And for our boys.*
Sempre primi di mi cuora

They gave this child more of themselves than that;
They gave him afterward every day—they became part of him
...
The family usages, the language, the company, the furniture—
the yearning and swelling heart,
These became part of that child who went forth every day,
and who now goes,
and will always go forth every day.
—Walt Whitman, "There Was a Child Went Forth"

# Contents

# Prologue

## The Journey to Parenthood

The sun slowly breaks over the misty hills in Sarria, a tiny village in the north of Spain. After a simple breakfast of bread, cheese and very strong coffee, our group gathers in the lobby and we set out for a small park on the edge of the path, where we often take time to meditate and set intentions for the day.

Michael and I have joined this group to walk the last hundred miles of the Camino de Santiago, a meandering path through farmland and hills across southern France and northern Spain, carved out by St. Jacques nearly nine hundred years before. The shoes of countless peregrinos, or spiritual pilgrims, have worn down this path.

Lisa, one of our guides and a gorgeous former dancer, leads us through a series of stretches to prepare our bodies for the long hike ahead. Then Abby and Stephen, our other guides, lead us through a meditation. Gently, Stephen encourages us to envision our dreams. Listening to his deep, soothing voice, my fears overwhelm me and tears fill my eyes. I struggle throughout my meditation to maintain calm; the challenges before me—both on the physical path and the path of my life—seem insurmountable.

As I shrug my backpack over my shoulders and fasten the harness around my waist, I whisper my prayer and intention over and over again: "I need your help. Please prepare me. Please prepare us."

We set off on the first nineteen-mile leg of our journey, on a path marked with shells at each half-kilometer. We stroll through farmlands and small villages, and everyone we pass smiles and wishes us a "*Buon' camino.*"

Walking together for hours can build a remarkable sense of camaraderie. Every one of us is drawn to this experience because we sense our lives are at some crossroads: new careers, relationships in crisis, family issues, major life choices that seem overwhelming. In the long hours we walk, we share meals, we talk, listen, and bond.

Michael and I have come to walk the Camino because we are about to bring children into our home. A year before, we'd started the adoption process with the county of Los Angeles, going through classes, a forty-page application, background checks, and home inspections where social workers clawed through every drawer and cabinet before we were approved to adopt.

After we were granted the stamp of approval, we'd waited months and months for the call. And finally, our social worker called, breathless and bit too perky, "I know you said you would were interested in one or possibly two children, but when I saw a report on this sibling set, I just knew they were for you."

She gave us a few sketchy details about their circumstances. "And I'm not supposed to say this, because every child is beautiful, but these kids are gorgeous. They'll take your breath away."

She paused for a moment. "But it's three boys. Biological brothers, ages twelve, nine and five. Should I give you a few minutes to make up your mind?"

Michael and I stared at each other across the speakerphone and finally spluttered that we'd get right back to her. Suddenly, the moment they told us about over and over in those excruciating classes had finally arrived. We might have a match.

Without a word, we'd telegraphed our thoughts back and forth. *We might be able to handle two, but three? Was the house big enough for all of us? Could we afford it? What if they didn't like dogs? What if they didn't like us?*

It was a surreal moment. We took each other's hands, closed our eyes, and said a prayer. It felt like the most natural and the only thing to do. Then I looked up at Michael and said, "These are our sons." And that was that.

A friend had e-mailed us about the group going on the Camino, and I knew we should go. I knew classes and inspections might qualify us to adopt, but no amount of homework could completely prepare the heart. So the Camino seemed like a good idea—a chance to ready ourselves before our lives changed forever.

Our fellow *peregrinos* are keenly interested in our prospective family. They ask probing, sometimes startlingly practical questions that make Michael and I think hard about the actual mechanics of running a family.

"How are you going to help them catch up at school?"

"What about the extra laundry and grocery shopping and carpooling?"

"How will you handle questions about being gay?"

"What are you going to do the first day you meet them?"

"What about the first time they stay overnight?"

As we sit on a hillside for morning meditation on the third day of our walk, Abby hands each of us a packet of seeds.

"I want you to sow your intentions by planting these seeds," she urges. "I want you to plant the seeds of whatever your heart desires."

I once again find myself overwhelmed: *God, what if I'm not a good father?*

Embarrassed, I walk away from the group to the edge of the park where we've gathered and look down over the small retaining wall. There, ten feet below us, is a small school building with a little playground, complete with swings, a slide, and monkey bars. *Is this a sign from the Universe?*

A laugh bubbles up, catching me by surprise, and my mood is lightened immediately. I drop my seeds onto the ground below, where I can see the small shoeprints of children who had played there the afternoon before, and I set my intention: that our transition as a new family is graceful and smooth, and that the bond of love comes quickly and easily.

As we walk, Michael and I develop contingency plans for every situation. And as we think and imagine and talk about what it will be like to face every new situation, something extraordinary begins to happen in my heart. I stop worrying about whether I am ready. Instead, I begin to acknowledge just how deeply and fully I want to bring these boys into our lives—I begin to trust the instinct already firmly planted in my soul to love them.

It feels like a small miracle that the dreams I record are no longer filled with fear and dread, but instead are small signposts of what might lie ahead. More miraculous still is the fact that on the hundred-mile journey, I never get a blister.

When we reach Santiago, the medieval university town where the Camino ends, we go to the cathedral to celebrate the Pilgrims' Mass with everyone else on the journey this week. The cathedral is packed with thousands, some still carrying their walking sticks, some still muddy and disheveled from the journey. When the brothers who serve at the church begin to swing enormous chalices filled with incense over our heads, I look across at my fellow *peregrinos* and begin to cry again—not from fear this time, but with joy as I look ahead to a new chapter in our lives.

Two weeks later, I sit down with my boss for my annual performance review, and a phrase comes tumbling from my mouth before I am even conscious I am speaking.

"I don't think I can do this anymore," I say, my face involuntarily contorting into a look of surprise. My boss' face mirrors my shock.

Suddenly, I become aware of a great battle that has been raging in some quiet place in my heart, far from my consciousness. In a flash, I see the dusty trail of the Camino and I know with great certainty that my path—that is, *our path as a family*—cannot include the demanding work I have been doing. Working eighty hours a week, juggling offices in Los Angeles and New York, would be so draining I would have nothing left to give to our boys.

My boss, herself a mother of three who had taken a leave of absence when her partner had given birth to their first child, understands my feelings perhaps better than I. She hugs me, offers me a generous severance, and wishes us well. And this, too, is another miracle of the Camino.

# Part I

## The Honeymoon

Making the decision to have a child—it's momentous. It is to decide forever to have your heart go walking outside your body.

*—Elizabeth Stone*

From the moment our social worker faxed over a picture of the boys, all grainy and dark, something shifted forever in my heart.

These were our sons.

In the first year, we crossed the hurdles of getting acquainted, discovering each other's habits, our likes and dislikes, and navigating together the cold bureaucracy of a social service system that required the boys to repeatedly appear in court.

In every moment, there was grace. The boys wanted to be with us, and we wanted to be with them. Our first year was a long, loving courtship that smoothed over all the potential rough patches.

Like any honeymoon, it was so rich we hoped it would last forever.

# First Visit

We pull up to the office and see her immediately—a gaunt figure in black, huddled on the curb, gnawing on a damaged piece of her bleached hair. "That's her," Michael says, nodding in her direction. "That's got to be her."

She doesn't look up as we walk past her into the building. I look back as we enter. I can see the curve of her spine and the outline of her ribs against her black blouse. "She doesn't look like she eats," I say.

"Drug addicts don't," Michael answers. "Do you think she knows who we are?"

"How could she?" I reply as I dial the extension of the social worker responsible for the three brothers we are adopting.

Carolina comes to the lobby immediately, jittery, her brown eyes wide. "I think their mother is under the influence. She just screamed at me that she'd get me for taking away her kids. I don't know how this visit will go."

"Is that her in the parking lot?"

Carolina looks out the door and nods. "Why don't you sit in the kitchen? When the boys arrive, I'll take them to the lawn right outside the kitchen windows, so you'll be able to observe how they interact without them seeing you."

Once the boys are ours, we'll have to decide if they will ever see their mother again. We are here to observe their interaction to help us decide.

We pull up two chairs and position them at the window. Michael takes my hand and squeezes it; we're both nervous about seeing our kids for the first time. A van pulls up and three boys tumble out, run to their mother, and throw their arms around her.

With Carolina in tow, they walk over to the lawn, settling under a tall eucalyptus tree. Mom stands stiffly and silently as the boys spin around her, calling out, "Mom, look at me!" and "Mom, see what I can do!" Exuberant, they jump and wrestle and roll on the lawn like puppies let out of a cage, performing for a mother who takes little notice of their joy.

This is the first time Michael and I have seen the boys in person. Michael is entranced; his eyes follow everything they do. "Did you see that? Look at how quick they are! They're so coordinated! They're great little athletes!"

He looks at me for a moment, worry on his face. "I just thought of something. I don't know how to play football. Do you?"

I shake my head, "My dad tried to make me, but I refused. I sort of liked being the sissy kid."

"I couldn't play—my asthma. Do you think we'll have to hire someone to teach us?"

"One of our friends has to know how," I answer.

The boys are hanging off the tree branches, swinging and jumping to the ground. Even though the window is closed, we can hear them laughing and shouting. No matter what they do, Mom doesn't move— her eyes are vacant, her body taut and tense.

My heart leaps to see the boys play, but my attention is riveted on the mother who is about to lose them. For the last three years, she battled to prove she was fit to raise her sons. But her addiction won out. She'd failed every drug test, dropped out of rehab, and done her best to avoid therapy. Her only contact with her children was in settings where she was watched and observed and judged. And here we are now, hidden by a window, watching the last chapter of a private family tragedy played out in public.

Suddenly, I feel guilty, as if I've rushed to the scene of a car wreck to see the Jaws of Life cut through metal to remove the bodies. "I feel like a voyeur," I whisper to Michael. "We don't have any business being here."

He squeezes my hand and says, "It doesn't feel comfortable. But think about how much seeing them might help us later on when the boys are missing her."

I nod, focusing on Mom again. Like a giant black maypole in an enchanted garden, she stands, oblivious to the life circling around her, suffocated and turned inward by the harsh, unforgiving demon that consumes her life.

As far as she knows, this is one of the last times she will see her sons. They know it, too. And as she stands, mute and helpless, they come to her, alone and together, to touch her and stroke her and hug her, murmuring the love and devotion only sons can give their mothers.

When the van pulls up again, the boys hug and pet and stroke her one last time before they drive away. She stands motionless until the van is out of sight, then crumbles in the parking lot like a broken doll. When Carolina moves to help her, she pushes Carolina off and slowly rises to her feet. She walks to her car and drives away.

The next day, Michael and I take the oldest boy to lunch so he can meet us for the first time. We walk toward him as he gets out of the van, and as soon as he realizes who we are, he looks a little startled. I whisper to Michael, "I think we're intimidating him." Our friend Belinda describes Michael as a Greek statue, and I'm pretty tall and big, as well. We tower over the boy as we shake hands, and he stares up at us, wide-eyed.

But he smiles shyly when Big Michael grins at him and says, "I think it's cool we have the same name."

"My real dad's name was Michael, too," he says. "I was named after him."

We brought pizza to eat in the park because Carolina had told us it was his favorite. He doesn't say much as we show him pictures of our house and our dogs and talk to him about a new life that could be his. He examines every picture like he is memorizing the details.

When we ask him if he wants to come live with us, he doesn't hesitate. Quietly, he says, "Yes." And then, in a rush, he tells us he wants his new life to be fun—he wants to skateboard and play football and go swimming every day.

Then his bright blue eyes cloud for a moment. "My mom is sick, and she can't take care of us," he says. "Will I still get to see her?"

Big Michael, who lost the mother he adored eight years ago, answers for both of us. "We know your mother loves you very much. And we know how much you love your mother. Of course you'll be able to see her."

He nods, taking it in. Then he says, "When you come next, will you bring your dogs?"

# Anxiety

"We still go to court tomorrow, right?" Little Michael asks no one in particular as he stares out the kitchen window. I nod, keeping my eyes on him as I load our dinner dishes into the dishwasher. Even though he and his brothers have settled in nicely with Daddy Michael and me, they've had a tough few weeks, and we know this looming court date is weighing on them. The court hearing will determine if their birth parents' parental rights will be terminated. It's the first step in the process of formally adopting them.

If their birth parents' rights are terminated, they officially become wards of the state and can be adopted. According to California law, they will have to live with us a minimum of six months before a formal adoption will be considered; we are jumping through one more hoop in a long series of hoops to make our new family legal.

In the State of California's eyes right now, Daddy Michael and I are just foster parents. But in our eyes, they are already our boys.

Michael, Dereck, and Matthew have been in our home for one month, and they seem to love living with our four dogs and us. The first night they were here, they hugged and kissed us goodnight, and they've done it every night since.

They were supposed to see their mother on supervised visits every Thursday. This last Thursday was only the second time she'd shown up. The prior visit, she'd been withdrawn and distant. She didn't even acknowledge that she had missed her oldest son's birthday two days before. The boys left that meeting sad and angry, and when they got into the car for this latest visit, they complained they didn't want to see her.

This time, however, she was bright and perky, even though she disappeared into the bathroom three times during their brief visit. Spending an hour and a half with a mother who seemed together and engaged made them happy. She called out, "I love you!" as they left, and they walked on air.

The bubble burst when they called her the next night. Her boyfriend, probably under the influence, answered. He screamed at and mocked the boys. He wouldn't let them talk to her. She called back very late that night, shouting into the phone, panting like a wild animal, asking the same questions over and over again.

When I told her the boys had gone to bed long before and were asleep, she couldn't understand why I wouldn't immediately wake them and bring them to the phone. "What's wrong with that?" she said. "What's wrong with that? What's wrong with that?"

The boys have a sixth sense about her and whatever state she is in, and they knew she'd called. Mom's boyfriend beat her, and they knew she sometimes didn't show up for their weekly visits because she didn't want them to see the bruises. When he wouldn't let them speak to her, they were afraid he'd done something terrible to her. They'd been on edge all weekend, fraught with worry.

Dereck, the middle boy, carried their collective anxiety physically. He threw up three times on Saturday and then took to his bed. Nearly catatonic for hours, he suddenly burst into tears and began to howl and scream late in the afternoon.

I'd held him as he cried, and I'd tried to soothe him. Finally, he choked out, "I think my mom's boyfriend is going to kill her." As soon as he said the words, he began to wail again, a horrible, deep cry of frustration and grief.

I knew he felt he needed to protect her, but he felt powerless to stop it. There was no soothing him; he walked around, stooped over like an old man, clutching his stomach for two days.

Now it is Sunday evening. The boys' misery levels have remained at red-alert the entire weekend. All Daddy Michael and I can do is hold and hug them and try to take their minds off their pain. The connection they feel to their mother is deep, and each of them—even the five-year-old—somehow feels responsible for taking care of her. To think something awful was happening to her yet be helpless to do anything about it was horrible for them.

Tomorrow we go to court. If she shows and tries to fight the court's action, the boys will be forced to take the stand and testify about their life with their mother. They know it, and so do I. None of us sleep well, unsure of what the next day will bring.

# Going to Court

Getting in the car to go to court, the boys are anxious. They associate court with bad memories, and the thirty-minute drive is tense and silent.

When the boys had seen their mother at their weekly visit the previous Thursday, she had told them and their social worker she planned to come to court and contest the decision to terminate her parental rights. When Carolina heard that, she had to gather the boys and tell them they might have to testify. "The judge will call you up, and he'll ask you a few questions," she said.

"But what if we don't want to say anything?" Dereck had wailed.

"I'm sorry, Dereck, but this is one of those times you won't have a choice. If your mom decides to fight, the judge will have to talk to each of you," she said gently. "But it won't be hard. The judge knows you may be uncomfortable, and he'll do everything he can to make it easy."

All the way to the court, Little Michael chews on his cuticles and Dereck chews his lip, both lost in thought. Even Matthew, still too young to quite understand, shares his brothers' anxiety, staring quietly out the window.

But there are some sweet surprises waiting for us when we get to the courthouse. The court-appointed attorney for the boys is a lesbian with a partner. They have just gone through the process of adopting their two children, and offers great pointers about how to proceed with the adoption. This is, of course, after she grills us about our intentions. She wants to be certain we are going to be fit parents for "these special boys," as she puts it.

Waiting in the hall to go into court, a woman carrying a briefcase stops and reintroduces herself to Daddy Michael. "Hey, do you remember that trip we were on together in Costa Rica?"

We talk for a few minutes before she asks, "What are you here for?" When we tell her we are here for a hearing to terminate the parental rights of the boys' birth parents, her eyes widen. "Oh, no. Are these Vicky's sons?"

When we nod, she excuses herself. "I'm so sorry. I didn't know. I'm not supposed to be talking to you. I'm Vicky's attorney!"

Moments later, our case is called, and we all walk into the courtroom. The judge watches as we walk the boys up to the front row, behind the attorneys, where the clerk indicates they should sit. Then we move to the rear of the courtroom, where we are told to go. He opens the proceedings and asks if the boys' mother is present. Checking around the courtroom, her attorney answers, "No."

The judge shakes his head sadly, and the attorney does her best to mask her own frustration. She asks the judge if she can use her time to address the court to convey a message to the boys from their mother. When he nods, she turns to them and says, "Your mom wants you to know how very, very much she loves you and how sad she is that she can't take care of you." We can see the boys' heads from behind, nodding as she finishes.

When she sits down, the judge asks if their birth father is in court. His court-appointed attorney says they have not been able to locate the father for some time, and he waives his time for comment.

The judge nods again and quickly rules to terminate the birth parents' rights. Looking at us sitting in the back of the courtroom, he says, "These boys are now free to be adopted."

All the anxiety and fear of the last three days lift as the judge pounds his gavel. As we walk out, Dereck takes my hand and says, "Can we get a hamburger? I'm hungry."

Even though it is just 10:30 in the morning, we drive to the boys' new favorite restaurant, The House of Pies, and giggle and laugh over hamburgers and chili cheese fries. We have crossed another hurdle.

# The Little Red Schoolhouse

"So where are you sending the boys to school?" my dentist Mitch asks as he starts scraping one of my molars. His assistant shoots a jet of water into my mouth, and I raise my eyebrows and shake my head slightly in reply to Mitch's question. The clock is ticking—the boys moved in at the end of July, and Michael and I have been so busy getting everyone settled, dealing with visitation (and the subsequent drama), and getting the boys to court that we hadn't addressed the school issue.

My gaze must convey the fact that we're in need of assistance, because Mitch says, "Call Ilise at the Hollywood Schoolhouse and tell her I sent you." I nod in agreement.

Mitch is our dentist and our friend. He and his partner Patrick adopted their two children through the county a few years ago. When we'd decided to go the same route, he'd recommended the social worker they'd worked with, a person who turned out to be a wonderful advocate for us also. We trusted Mitch's counsel because he knew firsthand what we were dealing with.

On the way home from Mitch's office, I drive by the Schoolhouse. It's a small private school on a busy street corner in the heart of Hollywood; the entire front of the building is painted fire engine red. It doesn't look like much from the street, but I know if Mitch recommends it, it has to be good.

The local public schools are abysmal, with test scores among the lowest in the state. The boys missed so much school when they lived with their birth mother, we know they won't stand a chance if they go into that kind of environment. It's one of the things we worry about the most. But with less than a month before classes are set to start, there doesn't seem to be much chance of getting them into a private school. And can we afford the tuition, on top of everything else?

When I get home, I call Ilise. On the phone, she is sweet and warm, and as soon as I mention Mitch, she goes on and on about how wonderful he is. "Bring the boys in," she says, "and let's do a tour. When do you want to stop by?"

"How about tomorrow morning?"

"Perfect. Ten o'clock?"

The boys are not happy about going to school in the morning. It's clear they don't associate school with anything positive; Michael hates taking tests, and Dereck is completely shut down, afraid to be in a new space. But when we walk into the reception area, everyone greets us warmly, and the boys began to relax a bit.

Ilise is everything Mitch said she'd be. She takes us on a tour of the school, which has students from preschool through eighth grade. The campus is a lot bigger than it looks from the street, and even though it's summer, we can sense that it's an environment designed to nurture kids.

As we walk, we tell Ilise about how we came to be a new family.

"You're just the kind of family we love to have at our school," she says, her eyes growing misty.

There are some obstacles, of course. The first grade class is already more than full, so there's a chance we'll have to enroll Matthew elsewhere.

But our biggest concern is that we can't afford private school tuition for all three boys. Michael and I have already worked the numbers until our fingers were numb; we might be able to afford tuition for one, and if we make some serious cost-cutting efforts, possibly two. But three? Impossible.

It was tough, but we had already worked out priorities for who would go to private school first. Given that Michael was the farthest behind academically and was already in middle school, we'd have less time to work with him and help him catch up. It made sense to make him top priority, academically. We'd just have to see how the other boys did in public school.

After our tour, we decide to have Michael take the admissions test right then and there. He goes into a testing room while we look over the application materials and meet with the interim head of school, Susan. She is just as warm as Ilise, and she tells us over and over how wonderful it is that we adopted the boys and kept them together.

When Michael finishes testing, Ilise encourages us to get our application in as quickly as possible. We go home to start working on the application materials and crunch the numbers one last time. I fret all night and even more as I drop off the application the next morning. How would all this work out?

We spend the next two days doing heavy research about the elementary schools nearby, trying to weigh all the information to determine which was the least likely to do the boys harm. Then Ilise calls and asks if we are free to come in for a follow-up interview. When we arrive, Ilise sits the boys in the waiting room and brings Michael and me into Susan's office.

Susan hugs us both and asks us to sit down. Smiling, she asks, "Well, are you still interested in coming to the Schoolhouse?" When we nod, she smiles and says, "Then I have a proposition for you."

Michael and I both lean forward.

"We think it is wonderful what you've done, and we really would like to have your family as part of the Schoolhouse community. We believe it would be really helpful for the boys as they adjust to their new life if they are all in the same school environment. We're willing to put Matthew in the first grade class, even though it's already full. We know the other parents would really support that choice."

She pauses, giving us a moment to process what she was saying.

"So here's our proposition. Would you be willing to enroll all three boys for the price of two?"

I sit back, stunned. She's offering us a full scholarship for one of the boys! I look over at Michael—I'm sure the incredulous look on his face is mirroring my own disbelief.

"Are you kidding?" Tears fill my eyes.

Susan laughs and comes over to hug us again. "Then we have a deal. Welcome to the Schoolhouse family."

Two weeks later, we line the boys up on the front steps for their first back-to-school picture, and then we drive them to class. All three of them look apprehensive as they reluctantly leave the shelter of the car and walk toward their new school. But Ilise and Susan are there to welcome them and usher them in.

When we pick them up at 3:30, three relaxed and happy boys are waiting. "How was school today?" I ask.

"Good," they all say. And I know they really mean it.

## New Name, New Life

From the day the boys moved in, friends and family from around the world have been sending gifts to welcome them. It's as if Christmas has come four months early—packages arrive every day, quickly filling their room with toys and goodies.

Dereck asks, "Who are Nate and Mary Ellen?" when a huge erector set arrived from Michigan one day. When toys and gummy bears arrived from Frankfurt, Little Michael wanted to know, "How do you know Cindy when she lives in Germany?"

As the boxes continued to arrive, I realized we had a problem. "Where are we going to put all this stuff?" I asked Daddy Michael. "There's no space left in their bedroom!"

He did the only thing he could—he took the van to Home Depot and returned with two long folding tables. We set them up in the only space big enough to hold all the loot: the garage. Soon, it looked like the stockroom at Toys 'R Us. As the tables filled with boxes and toys and goodies, I had to make a couple of trips to buy more thank-you cards.

Today we're writing those thank-you notes. The boys grumble and groan when I make them sit down to write to everyone. "Do we have to?" Little Michael complains.

"Yes," I say firmly. "Everyone who sent something made a special effort to pick out something you would like. Whenever anyone does something nice for you, you should always thank them."

Matthew looks up at me, his open grin showing his missing front teeth. "But I don't know how to write a letter," he said, hoping this would absolve him.

"Then you can draw a picture," I reply.

"Awww," he says.

All the boys love to draw, and they seem to have real ability. When I told this to my mom, who is a wonderful artist, she said, "That's it! Now I know what to get them!" Her package bearing art supplies and oil paints arrived just a few days later.

As they unpacked her gift, I told the boys how she taught me to draw when I was little. I remember sitting at the kitchen table with her while she worked with pastels on a large sheet, and I tried to copy what was doing on a small one.

Matthew now uses those art supplies to create his thank-you to my mom. He carefully draws a picture inside the card and hands it to Little Michael. As Little Michael writes "Dear Grandma" at the beginning of the note, Dereck looks up at me with a smile. "We never had a grandma before," he says. "This is cool!"

After the boys sign the card, they hand it back to me to put in the envelope. That's when I notice that Little Michael has signed his name "Michael Arden Sonego." It's the first time I've seen his new signature.

Later that night, as I check his homework, I notice a page in his language arts notebook where he's been practicing writing his new name over and over. With tears in my eyes, I show the page to Daddy Michael, and his eyes well with tears as well. Without ever saying anything to us, Little Michael has told us how he feels about being part of a new family.

## Just Stupid

Little Michael hunches over his math problems at the kitchen counter, his freckled face buried in his hands. "I can't learn this," he says over and over. "I'm just stupid." He's been in school for just two weeks, and he's struggling with his homework. We'd spent the last forty-five minutes on simple addition and subtraction problems, and we'd gotten nowhere.

When he finally looks up, there are tears in his eyes. It's the first time I've seen him cry. Earlier that day, after one of his brothers broke down after a sibling conflict, he'd proudly told me that even though his younger brothers often cried, he never did. But here he is now, big tears rolling down his cheeks, his face contorting in frustration and embarrassment.

I don't know what to do. I put my arm around his thin shoulders and hug him. This is not a stupid kid, although he consistently tests below average for his age and grade. I'd watch his mind fly around new concepts in math, catching subtleties that I had to think twice about before I understood. So what is the problem? There is some block that prevents him from learning, and we need to figure out what it was.

As I hold him and he continues to cry, my mind flashes to the first time I had really struggled in school. I was in kindergarten at St. Ignatius Loyola, and I'd missed more than a week of class because I had the chickenpox.

The day I returned, Sister Henrietta Marie beat my hands with a wooden ruler because I didn't know my colors—everyone else in the class learned them while I was sick. "You're just a stupid, stupid boy," she said as she pummeled my stinging palms.

I'd burned with shame. When I came home at the end of the day, I cried in front of my mother and told her what happened. With three small children in diapers, she had little time for sympathy. "That's just the way those nuns are," she said.

From that day on, I'd hide my shoes in the backyard or bury my school clothes under the bed so I wouldn't have to go to school, and my poor mother had to struggle to get me dressed and out the door each morning.

"Michael, didn't you miss a lot of school when you were younger?" He nods slowly. His social worker had told us he missed more than

14

sixty days of school for a couple of years in a row while living with his birth mom. He'd been held back a year to make up for those lost days.

"Well, I bet you missed a lot of math when you were out, didn't you?" He nods again. "So it makes sense you never learned how to do addition and subtraction. You probably missed it when you weren't in school." He nods yet again, and I know I am on the right track.

"Well, there's a big difference between being stupid and just not having been in school to learn something everyone else did. We've been working on math homework now for the past few weeks, and I can see that whenever you learn something new in class, you immediately figure out the homework. That tells me you are really smart. But when you have to rely on knowledge they assume you learned in school before, you have a hard time. That tells me you never got to learn those things in the first place."

This catches his attention, and he wipes the last of the tears from his eyes.

"So you've been beating yourself up and telling yourself you're stupid because you don't know things you never got to learn. It's not your fault you missed so much school and didn't learn how to do addition and subtraction."

He gulps and nods again. I realize this is the first time someone has ever told him he isn't responsible for the painful things that have happened to him in his young life. "I just feel stupid because everybody else knows things I don't."

"I'm sorry you feel that way, Michael, because I know you're not stupid. You just didn't get to learn as much as some other kids your age, but all that means is you're going to work a bit harder just to catch up. If you decide you want to do it, I know you can."

He nods in agreement and picks up his pencil again. He finishes his problem set in record time, and we have a bowl of vanilla ice cream with chocolate syrup to celebrate.

While the war with math isn't over yet, a decisive battle has been won. Week by week, Michael begins to gain confidence in his skills and relies less and less on the little addition and subtraction cheat sheets we've created.

The day he brings home a 94 percent on his first math test, he has a wry grin on his face. "I did better than any of my friends," he says.

For one of the first times in his life, he is ahead of the curve—and the dad who still sees himself as the little kindergartener with the bright red palms can't help but grin right along with him.

# A Death in the Family

Little Michael has a look of panic on his face as he dashes into my office. "There's something wrong with Celeste." Our eight-year-old Old English Sheepdog is a gentle, sweet, cuddly bear of a dog, blind since she was four months old. We have a special bond, Celeste and I, and every morning she sticks her nose in my face to tell me it is time to get up.

I run with Little Michael into the garage and discover Celeste lying on the floor in the farthest corner, her nose pressed against the cabinet. Panting, her chest heaving, she is clearly struggling.

I bend down to check her, speaking to her softly. Her heartbeat is erratic, her stomach distended. I turn to Little Michael.

"Honey, go get my car keys. They're on my dresser. Hurry." Michael turns and runs, tears filling his eyes. The other boys stand in the doorway, eyes wide and fearful.

Celeste's tongue is turning blue—not enough oxygen. I stick my finger in her throat, just in case she's swallowed something. She gags, but her throat is clear. I don't understand what's wrong. Just minutes before, she was leaning against me in the kitchen, nudging for me to scratch her ears. Like every other night, she'd nearly swallowed her dinner whole and went scavenging in the other dogs' bowls to find remnants. After a few contented belches, she'd settled down to snore near the dining room table. There was nothing wrong with her.

Little Michael is back, keys in his hand. "Dereck, open the garage door," I say as I begin to lift Celeste into my arms. As I stand with my hundred-pound dog clutched to my chest, her front paws stiffen and she gasps one last time. Her head rolls back, and she is gone.

I start screaming. "No, Celeste, no! Don't die! Don't die on me!" The boys are wailing now. Hoping against hope, I put her body in the back of the car. "Boys, I'm going to take her to the vet. Maybe it's not too late. Wait here."

I know it's too late, but I can't stop myself from driving on a fruitless journey to the emergency vet.

Later, I bring her body back home with me. The vet was sympathetic, but there was nothing he could do. After hearing what happened, he told me that occasionally big dog's stomachs will suddenly turn after eating a big meal. It puts pressure on the lungs and heart, and within minutes, they can die. This was probably what happened with Celeste. He offered to dispose of her, but I can't bear to leave her there; our regular vet will take care of the cremation tomorrow, and I want to have her body with us for one last night at home.

Daddy Michael and the boys are all waiting, all crying, all in shock. "They couldn't do anything," I choke out as I, too, begin to sob.

We stand in the garage, huddled together, crying uncontrollably.

Every dog is special, I know, but Celeste had been extraordinary. I'd gotten her at six weeks, a chubby black-and-white sheep dog, looking more like a little round panda than a puppy. As she grew, she began to run into things—she'd charge into a wall or a piece of furniture like she hadn't seen it. And indeed, she hadn't. She had a rare genetic disorder, and her retinas had already disintegrated. Born with sight, she was completely blind just four months later.

The breeder offered to replace her—in fact, she demanded it, noting she had the right to destroy a defective animal. It was in the contract we had signed. But I refused. Her blindness did not make Celeste defective to me—only more special.

Every time I moved into a new house, I would put her on a leash and walk her through so she'd get to know the terrain. It would only take one time for her to catch on. She traveled with me, through house after house, even on a move across the country and into a new relationship with Michael and then as we adopted children. She was always loving, always steadfast, and always adaptable to the new circumstances that came her way.

As she grew older, she would wait by the side of our bed each morning for the alarm to go off before tentatively climbing up and plopping down between Michael and me. She would press against us while we cuddled and talked to her. She would moan with pleasure, relaxed and content, knowing she was safe and deeply loved.

When the boys came to our home, she immediately accepted them as part of the family. She clearly loved them, sensing their energy and enjoying the noise and activity in the house. She knew each by voice, licking their faces when they bent down to cuddle and kiss her, often happy to lie at their feet while they played. And they loved her, too, nicknaming her "Celeste, the Best."

Later, as we get the boys ready for bed, we decide to sit together on the floor of their room and say a prayer for Celeste. Mo, our shepherd mix, sits between Dereck and I, her mournful eyes telling us she knows what has just happened. As we join hands, Dereck holds one of Mo's paws and I take the other. We cry as we ask God to bless Celeste and thank him for giving her to us.

In the morning, the mood is somber as I drive the boys to school. That afternoon, when I come home after a long meeting downtown, I find a big sign taped to the front door. In bright blue pen on green construction paper is written,

*Papa, we're so sorry. We loved Celeste, but we know you loved Celeste more.*

*Love, your sons Michael, Dereck, and Matthew.*

I stand there, holding my briefcase and crying until they open the door, running to hug me and bring me into the house.

## Losing a Mother's Love

I was twelve when my Aunt Joy walked out on her husband and four boys. She told her horrified sisters, "I can't do this anymore." And for the rest of her life, she refused to say why she left with nothing but the clothes she was wearing.

She never saw her boys again. Once my uncle realized Joy was not coming back, he packed everyone up and moved two thousand miles away to California, and they were lost to our family. As she got older, Aunt Joy attempted to make contact, but they wanted nothing to do with her. They could not—or would not—forgive her.

Thirty years later, when she got sick with the lung disease that finally took her life, she made her sisters and her second husband promise not to tell her boys until after she was gone. There would be no deathbed reconciliation for her.

Aunt Joy died in November 2004, painfully struggling to breathe to the last. My mom had seen her just days before and cried as she told me how Joy had clutched her and whispered, "I'm ready" as they said good-bye. She was my mother's closest sister and her best friend, and to hear my mother cry broke my heart. But I grieved more for my mother's sorrow than the news itself. Joy was my favorite aunt when I was young, but that changed when she left her children. I never saw her the same way again.

When mom asked me to try to find her sons to tell them, I couldn't say no. I knew very little about them. Their lives in California had not been easy. My uncle had remarried and become a drunk. The boys got into trouble with the law. One had served time in prison for armed robbery. But I found three of their names and phone numbers on the Internet and thought about what I would say to them after more than thirty years.

The last time I saw them, they were probably close to the ages of our boys, who had moved in three months earlier.

Just thirty days after our boys came, the court had terminated their mother's parental rights. Her drug addiction and refusal to follow through on treatment, along with record of seven arrests over seventeen years for possession and sale, worked against her. It didn't help that she didn't show up at court on the day they were to consider termination. With a track record like that, no court would dream of giving her kids back to her.

The boys had not seen her since, and they'd taken to their new home and new life like fish to water. They'd embraced our friends and family and dogs, and it was clear they'd become attached to us. Every morning, when they climbed out of the car at school, they all grabbed my head and kissed my cheek before scampering onto the playground. When we sat together to watch TV, Daddy Michael and I formed the base of a big pile of intertwined kids and dogs. In such close quarters, they all went to sleep quickly. Sometimes we couldn't hear the TV over the sounds of snoring dogs and kids.

Despite all this, their mom is always present in their lives. Driving by a corner gas station with a convenience store attached, Little Michael tells me, "My mom used to buy me breakfast there every morning before school." At the grocery store, Dereck asks if we can get mint chocolate chip ice cream. That night, he refuses to eat it. He doesn't really like mint chocolate chip. He chose it because it was his mother's favorite.

Last week, during her monthly home visit, their social worker asked if they wanted to see their mother again. They all responded brightly, "Yeah!" But after she left, Dereck climbed onto his bed and spent two hours staring at the wall, refusing to talk. And Little Michael told me, "I don't really want to see my mom. I'm mad she didn't try hard enough to keep us." Their anguish at being abandoned is palpable.

They can't always talk about it, but it shows up in their behavior. When we try to work in the office when they are home, they hang on our chairs, clinging with all the fierceness they can muster. If we run out of milk and I need to go to the store, they have to go, too—they all try to climb on my back at once, wanting a piggyback ride through the aisles. When we go to a movie, they want to sit in the middle, with Daddy Michael and me on either end like protective bookends.

From the first week they were with us, they would constantly squeeze our biceps or poke our stomachs or demand, "Put me on your shoulders!" After what felt like the millionth poke, I complained to our friend Belinda that I felt like a horse about to be traded.

"Oh, sweetie," she said. "Don't you see? They want to make sure you're strong enough to protect them from getting hurt again. They want to feel safe."

Since the court terminated her rights, their mother has called against court orders more than once, tearfully asking us to put her sons on the phone. When we tell her we can't let her speak to them, she always pleads, "Please tell them how much I love them."

I hear the sorrow in her voice, and it could make my heart break. But I also see the mix of pain and love and anger in the children she bore, the boys who are now our sons. At times I am angry, thinking the damage has been done and she's lost any right to have a presence in the boys' lives.

But as I pick up the phone to call my cousins, I think of the woman who closed a door thirty years ago and never had the opportunity to make amends. She, and her sons, suffered for it. I don't want that to happen with my boys.

# Consequences

Daddy Michael and I collapse on the bed, and I stare out the window. The early winter sunset casts long shadows on the mountains in the distance, rose and crimson fading into deep purple. Normally, the sight would make me sigh with joy. Today, I barely notice.

It's Sunday afternoon, and we feel worn out and beat down. We're in day three of a four-day weekend. Each day the boys have been home, the level of acting out and bad behavior has increased. The boys' lives have been buffeted by circumstances beyond their control, but they've found safety in a daily routine since school started. Holidays are unavoidable, though; and since the long weekend is unstructured, it creates space for their anxieties and fears to emerge. Little things send them careening into dark emotional waters.

The stress comes out in small, malicious ways. This morning, when we got into the car to go shopping and then to football practice, Dereck jumped into his seat and quickly snapped his seatbelt into place. Matthew had to climb over the middle of the seat to the back row of the minivan to get to his seat. Dereck wore a tight, small smile as he watched Matthew scramble—Dereck had used the power of his age and size to torment his little brother.

Later, when they were playing together on PlayStation, we heard a ruckus. We came in to see Matthew crumpled on the floor, crying. Dereck sat, grasping both controls in his hands with bright red patches burning on his cheeks, that same smug smile covering his face. Matthew choked out that it was his turn, and he had scored a touchdown when Dereck grabbed his control and started the game over, angry because Matthew was winning. Dereck said flatly, "He's lying. He was pressing all the buttons on my control!"

Exasperated, I wrapped up the controls and put them away. I knew one of them was lying, and I'd have put money on it being Dereck. Until one of them admitted the lie, PlayStation would be off limits. Derek wrapped his arms around himself, a stubborn child Sphinx, refusing to speak. We told him he must go to his room until he was ready to participate in conversation again.

He stomped off to his room, furious at being punished. Just a few minutes later, Matthew came to us to tell us that Dereck had lied. Could he play with PlayStation again? I checked in with Dereck, asking if he

23

had something to tell me. He barely shook his head, still on his silent strike, and I could see from Matthew's face he isn't telling the truth.

The greatest frustration for me is that I don't know how to fix their behaviors and the feelings behind them. And while Dereck and Matthew continue to battle, Little Michael is dealing with even bigger challenges. Last week, his teachers contacted us to tell us that his work had dramatically fallen off.

After a stellar 94 percent on his first math test, he received a D- on this week's test. Mr. Narbe, his math teacher, tutors Michael after school every week—he told us he didn't believe Michael had even tried to do well. He was also having problems in other classes; he failed to write any answers on the last page of his Spanish test, and he'd earned a detention in social studies for failing to do his homework and an in-class assignment.

Little Michael has begun to give up whenever things get tough. Facing some new concept in his homework is enough to make him chew his nails and pace the floor. Despite the fact that he loves his new school, he still sees schoolwork as a chronic form of punishment for his failures. He missed so much school in his early years, there are huge gaps in his learning. Perpetually behind, he tends to zone out whenever he decides the work is too hard.

Last night, Daddy Michael and I summoned him into the small home office we share just off the master bedroom. Michael knew we'd been talking to his teachers, and his face was worried.

When I closed the door, he looked up and asked, "Am I in trouble?" Michael is sensitive, so our approach was gentle. "You know how important your schoolwork is, and we see you working hard on your homework. But Mr. Narbe and Ms. Laira are both telling us that your work has slipped. Mr. Narbe told us you got a D- on your math test on Monday. We know you studied—what happened when you took the test?"

Embarrassed, he shrank into his chair, rubbing his eyes with his hands. He kept saying, "I don't know. I don't know." We've learned that Michael needs time to process things before he can respond, so I told him he should think about what had happened and what he needed to do, and we would discuss it later in the weekend.

"We want you to be successful in school. And we know you can be," Daddy Michael said gently.

"Your schoolwork is your most important priority now," I added, continuing his thought. "And if you aren't devoting enough time or energy to it, other things might have to be cut out so that you can."

This got Little Michael's attention: he's dying for a drum set for Christmas, and he plays on a tag football team twice a week. "We might have to wait on the drum set and stop football until you can get your grades back up," I added. Hearing that, his face fell even more.

The conversation left Little Michael in a foul mood. During football practice, Michael jammed his finger when he caught a pass. When he complained, his coach had checked his finger to see if it was sprained or broken. His finger seemed fine, so the coach sent him back onto the field. Angry that he didn't get more sympathy, Michael decided to quit right then and there. He walked away from practice, sulking on the sidelines until we picked him up. Once we got home, he rocked in a chair, staring at his bruised finger and glowering miserably as his brothers fought in the background.

I was at my wits' end. For the first time, I began to understand what drove my mother so crazy when we were kids. She was overwhelmed by the nonstop demands of raising five children. Dealing with the three sulking monsters before me, I couldn't even begin to imagine what her life must have been like.

Feeling completely overwhelmed, I realized I needed to give myself a break. I snapped one more order: "You guys play in your playroom. We're going up to our room because we need a time out. Don't bother us unless there's an emergency."

Michael and I climbed the stairs, closed the door, and lay on the bed, silent, weary, and frustrated.

We could still hear them, shouting as they tossed their football in the playroom, but the din was distant enough to give us a momentary reprieve. I closed my eyes and prayed the only words I can manage, "Help me." I wanted my mind and heart to settle. And slowly, as I breathed deeply, a quiet peace began to nibble away at my frustration. We both fell asleep.

*****

Sometimes, sleeping on a problem is the best way to come to a solution. So many times when something has been eating at me, I've learned to ask for help before going to sleep. My mind continues to work while

25

my body rests; almost always, an answer—or at very least, a next step—comes to me as I wake.

I sleep for just a few minutes when something flashes in my head. What had I wanted most from my beleaguered mother when I was their age? She had five kids to deal with. She was always so busy with cleaning and laundry and cooking and trying to maintain some semblance of order in a chaotic house, she didn't have time to coddle us.

I can still remember the positive things she said to me as a child. She told me I could draw. She told me I was smart. She told me I was a good helper when I cleaned the house. And she taught me to read while she was potty training me, so she could leave me alone for a few minutes while she watched the other kids.

I realize those four behaviors continued to define how I see myself today. No one cleans a house better than I do. I still approach problem solving with a confidence—I can figure anything out if I need to. I am a voracious reader to this day, and the bathroom is still my reading sanctuary. I can't brush my teeth or shave without propping up a book on the back of the toilet.

I counted on mom to tell me good things about myself, and I believed her when she said them. Any time she said something positive, I walked on air and would have done cartwheels to please her. When she said something negative, I would sulk and act out, feeling miserable. Invariably, I would do something else that would make her mad.

We'd been hard on the boys all week, chasing after them to clean up their messes, to be more responsible for their homework, to stop bickering. What they heard from us, while not driven by rage, was consistently negative. Instead of inspiring better behavior, we had set the tone for further mischief.

If we are going to change the pattern, we need to reframe our interaction. I open my eyes and look over at Michael. He, too, is awake.

"I've just figured something out," I tell him. Sometimes, we speak in shorthand, and this is one of those times; he quickly gets it. We pray together and ask for help raising our boys.

While I make dinner, I tell them I want to have a family conference around the table.

"So the first item on the agenda," I tell them once they are all seated, "is for each of us to go around the table and share three things we liked about everyone sitting there."

The boys giggle, but they get right into it. All three like Daddy Michael and I because we play with them and take them places; I make good food and Daddy Michael tells funny jokes. And they don't have to work hard to say nice things about each other.

"Do you think you know what we expect of you?" I ask next. They all nod their heads. "I'm going to write down the things you tell me, and that's going to be the basis for family rules, okay?" They nod again.

Dereck speaks first. "You want us to be gentlemen." When I ask him what that means, he says, "Be nice to each other and to other people, and don't burp and fart at the dinner table."

We all laugh, and they quickly come up with twelve other things that define good behavior in our household. They cover everything from doing homework to making their beds to feeding the fish. There is no question they know what we expect of them.

The next subject: consequences of bad behavior. When I ask if they understand the meaning of the word "consequences," Matthew pipes up, "Ms. Cori talks about consequences in class." When I ask what consequences means, he says, "Like when we have a time out if we talk too much."

"So if you don't do the things you've put on this list, what do you think the consequences should be?" I ask.

"No PlayStation," they answer, almost in unison.

"Okay," I say. "That's a good consequence. But sometimes not being able to play PlayStation might be too severe. Are there other consequences you could think of?" They quickly come up with a few more, and we laugh and giggle through the rest of dinner, teasing Little Michael when he farts repeatedly.

After they go to bed, I type up their expectations and consequences lists, and Monday morning, they gather in our office for a solemn signing ceremony. And then we go back downstairs to make breakfast.

It's the last day of their four-day weekend, and while they still bicker and continue to act out, there is a lightness that had not been there the day before. Maybe it's because Daddy Michael and I aren't so tense and ready to pounce every time they do something wrong; maybe it's because they're not as high-strung as they had been the previous three days. Or maybe it was because they, and we, are feeling a just little safer and better understood.

## Teenage Hygiene

Come Christmas break, we have different challenges. On day two of the holiday vacation, Michael and I have a quick whispered conference. "Does Little Michael smell funky to you?" he asks me.

I nod. "It's not just he doesn't smell clean. It smells like he's fermenting. I know he changed his clothes, but did he take a shower yesterday?"

"I'm not sure."

"Me either. Do you want to talk to him, or should I?" Daddy Michael nods at me, and I'm appointed.

Little Michael is lying on his bed, staring into space. His hair, which we've let him grow out since he's lived with us, is matted and clumpy; he's wearing the clothes he slept in. His glasses are askew on his face, twisted up on one side. Even though it is nearly noon, his bed is still unmade.

"What are you doing, Michael?"

"Nothing."

"Have you taken a shower today?"

He shakes his head.

"How come?"

"I don't feel like it."

"Why not?"

"Dunno." He turns his head away, not wanting to continue the conversation.

I sit down on the edge of the bed. "Honey, I have to tell you something. You're starting to smell."

He turns his head back to look at me. "No, I'm not."

"Both Michael and I have noticed. You may not notice, but others around you do. You're thirteen, and at the age when your body is starting to change and your hormones are kicking in. That triggers changes in how your body smells. And when you aren't clean, the smell is pretty strong. So it is important to wash and keep yourself clean."

"I don't feel like it. My head hurts." Claiming to have a headache is always Michael's first line of defense whenever he doesn't want to do something.

"This isn't something you can negotiate. You need to take a shower now."

He glowers at me, but gets up and goes into the bathroom.

Over the five months he's been with us, we've seen him fall into depressions where he sits and stares. But the refusal to shower is new.

The holiday week between Christmas and New Year's has been a tough week for him. Without the structure his school schedule provides, he doesn't know how to fill his time. He alternates between manic play with his younger brothers and lying on his bed, staring into space. As each day passes, the periods on the bed lengthen.

We can coax him off the bed with an offer of something fun to do, but we are still concerned. He's going through so many transitions at once. His body is growing and changing in ways that are new and unfamiliar. He's moved into a new home with two dads. He's enrolled at a private school where all his peers are high achievers, and he struggles with making up the big holes in his past education. And, of course, he's slowly recognizing how deeply angry he is with his mother. He says over and over, "She didn't try hard enough to keep us."

We watch him play, and it often seems like he is reverting, behaving more like a nine- or ten-year-old than a boy of thirteen. I've been reading about the behavior of children of addicts, and sadly, Michael's behavior isn't unusual.

As the oldest, he was expected to be responsible for his brothers, taking care of them whenever his mom was out of it, without ever really knowing for himself what it was like to be cared for consistently. It's a double whammy for a young boy—saddled with responsibility at an early age without ever getting the love and attention he needed. It's the perfect recipe for creating a child who feels inadequate, worthless, and of little value; depression and self-neglect are the direct result.

On New Year's Eve we talk about making resolutions. For some reason, the boys think resolutions have to do with a choice of future career. Matthew immediately pipes up with, "My resolution is that I want to be a policeman when I grow up."

Dereck follows. "I want to be a professional football player."

Michael smirks and says, "I want to be a couch potato."

As the three boys erupt in giggles, Daddy Michael and I look at each other across the table sadly. How can we give a boy who feels worthless the wherewithal to find his own value?

Those feelings show up in myriad ways. He gives up when things are too hard; he feels inferior to the other boys in his class, so he holds back and doesn't make friends with the boys who have gone out of their way to include him; he can be aggressive about asserting his rights, but that assertiveness collapses if he's challenged. When he's angry about something, he becomes silent, turning the anger inward, his eyes clouded and his mouth set in a severe frown.

More than his brothers, I worry about Little Michael and how he will make it in the world. So much damage has already been done.

His struggles get deeply under my skin. I remember another boy of thirteen, reliving the agony of sprouting facial hair and a changing voice. My mom, whose eyesight was as bad as mine but hated wearing glasses, even noticed the spiky hairs protruding from my chin. "What's that fuzz on your face?" I was so mortified that when I opened my mouth, nothing could come out.

We moved three times in the interminable period when my voice changed. It cracked and trailed away every time I tried to speak. Starting in two new junior high schools was the most excruciating experience of my life; imagine trying to tell your school counselor what classes you want to take and not being able to get the words out. For months, I was silent, afraid of the cackles that erupted whenever I tried to make a sound.

That was the year I started going to Mass every morning before school, leaving the house before anyone else was up. I knew God could hear my prayers, even if they didn't sound right when they came out. That was also the year I went to Christmas Eve service and walked home to find my family had already opened all their presents and gone to bed. My gifts were left in a pile near the Christmas tree. No one should ever feel so alone.

I remember this and more as I watch my son. I can't take away the pain of his past or the confusion he feels today, but I can hug him and hold him and let him know that no matter how bad he feels, he is deeply loved. As I share with him the love he deserves, the confused, scruffy-faced boy on the brink of manhood who is still in my memory smiles and knows that he, too, is feeling loved. Healing and grace abound.

# Exposure

Our friend Anthony has taken me aside twice this week to tell me he has used crystal meth again. At lunch today, he whispers so the boys and Daddy Michael won't hear. "I used a little at midnight last night and was up until four. And I keep hearing voices when I walk around the house and drive in the car."

I squeeze his forearm in support, my face a mask. Anthony is one of the most important people in our lives, someone we've shared meals with three or four times a week since Michael and I have been together, one of the rare people we know we can count on whenever we need anything.

Anthony is a retired anesthesiologist, a brilliant, creative man with an enormous curiosity about life and an enormous love of learning. He was forced to retire from his practice ten years ago when he was diagnosed with HIV. It was a bitter blow to a proud man who took enormous pride in his work; he has struggled to keep up his spirits and sense of purpose. He was drawn into recreational drug use partially out of boredom and partially out of sense that his days were numbered.

"Why not enjoy myself?" he'd said to me more than once.

But the drug use quickly became a black hole that threatened to consume him. He's binged and then worked hard to stay clean so many times already, and each round of abuse has taken its toll. I'm afraid that if he falls into a pattern of using again, it could trigger another downward spiral that might take weeks or months to work out. Too many times over the past few years, we've watched the rapid disintegration of his body and spirit, and we've wondered if he would pull through the latest cycle of abuse.

Anthony and Michael have been friends for more than twenty years. He's always had a paternal feeling toward Michael, and when Michael invited him to dinner shortly after we first started dating, my new partner warned me to expect an interrogation.

I love to cook, but this was one of the first times in my life I was nervous working in the kitchen. I was more than a bit intimidated and afraid I might not pass muster.

As we ate, Anthony quizzed me mercilessly about my life and background, never once saying anything about the course after course I'd laid out. But something must have satisfied him, because after dinner, he told us to relax near the fireplace while he sat at the piano and serenaded us. He left after signing five songs he'd picked especially for the occasion, and from that night on, Anthony was one of my best friends, too.

When Michael and I began to plan our commitment ceremony, we asked him if he would toast us. At first he said no, because he has a great fear of speaking in public, but he thought about it for a few days and came back to us and said, "I'd consider it an honor."

His toast brought us and many of the people in the audience to tears. As a special gift to me, he found a beautiful ceramic piece that Michael's mother had created just before she died and gave it to me, because he knew she would want me to have something she had made.

But this beautiful, thoughtful man struggles with demons. When he uses, the drugs combine with his HIV meds to trigger terrible paranoia. He thinks his neighbors are out to harm him; he believes his friends will betray him; he thinks spirits haunt his house and want to hurt him. There are nights when he sits on his couch wrapped in a blanket with a baseball bat in his hand, waiting for the attacks he feels certain will come.

Anthony has always had dreams that involve monsters and blood—they are almost always cast in vivid reds. Some of his HIV meds amplify the terror of his dreams, and when he uses, the dreams become even more violent and make him even more afraid.

The combination of the meth and the fear of what could happen to him while he sleeps keep him from getting the rest his body needs. He grows haggard, and he speaks in a loud and rapid staccato, as if a flurry of words will keep the demons away. He paces endlessly until his body finally gives out and he collapses in exhaustion.

Before the boys came to us, he sometimes took refuge on our couch, where he could sleep feeling relatively safe. Sensing he needed to be watched, our dog Mo would often leave her post near our bed to curl up on the floor next to him. I'd find them together, Anthony's hand resting on her back, both in an uneasy rest. Mo kept an eye trained on Anthony as he worked the drugs and dreams out of his system. Sometimes, he would sweat so much from the exertion he'd leave an outline of his body on the cushions.

When we told our friends we wanted to adopt, Anthony was our greatest advocate. He loves kids. His nephews and nieces worship him. He's got a great playful streak in him, and he is a great teacher—a combination that makes him seem like the Pied Piper.

From the first, the boys loved Uncle Anthony. He burst into the house, ablaze with energy and ready to quiz them on state capitals or wildflowers. He introduced them to their favorite book, *Walter the Farting Dog*, and teased them in a way neither Michael nor I can.

Every time he pulls into the driveway, the boys scream "Uncle Anthony!" and careen to the front door to greet him. It tugs at my heart every time. They are so pure in their love for him. But they've known what it means to lose someone because of their addiction. How deeply would they be wounded again if something happens to Anthony?

It's a terrible dilemma. More than once before the boys met Anthony, I wondered if we needed to create some distance between him and our new family; I didn't want even a hint of drug use to mar their lives again. But just before the boys moved in, he came to the house, more upset and despondent than I'd ever seen him. His sister-in-law had told him that if she could tell he used again, she would never again allow him to have any contact with his nieces.

When he sat down on our couch, his big, muscular shoulders were slumped, and he could barely look at me as he repeated her words. "I don't know what I would do if I couldn't see them again," was all he could say.

"Did you use when you were with them?" I asked.

"I would never do that," he said, and I believed him. I knew he would keep the same commitment around our boys, and I knew then he would continue to be an important part of our new family, just as he had always been an important part of my and Michael's life together.

So Anthony comes to dinner every week or so, and on the weekends, we often meet him for breakfast at his favorite dive. After dinner, when it's time for Matthew to go to bed, Anthony will often tell him a story that he's woven from his great and wonderful imagination. As I stand in the doorway watching Matthew listen in rapt attention, I can't help but murmur a prayer of gratitude for Anthony's gift to our children.

On a Friday night last month, after we all sat down at the table for dinner and held hands and said grace, Anthony stood up with his glass of water in his hand, and said, "I want to make a toast." The boys started giggling, anticipating Uncle Anthony would tell one of his funny stories.

But he surprised everyone. His eyes got a little wet as he raised his glass and said very simply, "I want to thank Michael and John for letting me be part of this wonderful family and for Matthew, Dereck, and Michael for making me feel so welcome." We all clinked our glasses and drank.

Then he sat down, and with a mischievous grin, looked across the table and said, "Alright, Dereck, what's the capital of Michigan?"

## Living in a Circle of Prayer

Our friend Dirk is in the hospital again, gravely ill. Just two months ago, he spent weeks in intensive care, his kidneys refusing to function, the poisons in his body robbing him of the energy he needed to pull through. His many friends organized a prayer chain and a round-the-clock bedside vigil, slowly and steadily coaxing him back to life.

He left the hospital then with a shunt in his stomach to draw out the poisons. He was filled with resolve, certain his wasted kidneys would one day work again. He would overcome the HIV virus that stripped his immune system and had contributed to his kidneys' failure, and he would resume a healthy life. We were all heartened by his valor, thankful he seemed to be getting better.

And now, after a series of seizures, he lies in the hospital again. An infection formed around the hole in his stomach. As the infection raced through his body, it somehow triggered seizures. In the hospital, he developed pneumonia and a blood clot. Over the past five days, he has hovered between life and death, his fever racing and his spirits low.

We met Dirk when he learned about our new family from our mutual friends Abby and Stephen. When Abby called to tell us Dirk wanted to come and lead children's games at Little Michael's birthday party, we immediately said yes. Within minutes of his arrival, all twenty kids were clustered around him, laughing, playing, and following along as he led them through hours of magic and games.

That is Dirk's gift: he is the magic man. He brings light and joy to everyone around him, he reminds us how important it is to look at the world with childlike innocence and wonder.

And he is a spiritual healer. He can intuit where there is something in a body or a soul that must be addressed. At the party, he put his hand on my shoulder and said, "Honey, you are carrying the weight of the world. Sit down for a second." My boys watched, fascinated, as he poked and prodded along my neck and spine; I felt the hot energy emanating out of his hands as he lifted hard boulders of worry and tension from my aching shoulders.

The first time Dirk was in the hospital, the boys made him a get-well card, telling him they loved him and wanted him to get better.

When he was released, they were overjoyed. But even then, I felt an intuitive foreboding that something was not right.

Since Dirk has gone back into the hospital, Stephen has taken on the role of Dirk's chief caretaker. He sits with him for hours, tending to his needs; he sends out daily e-mail updates and was the one who enrolled Dirk's friends in a constant prayer circle to send him light and love. When it seems to Stephen that Dirk is ready to slip away, he whispers in his ear, cajoling him and telling him there is no way he can die yet.

As Stephen tells me about the time he spends with Dirk, I ask a blunt question: "Does Dirk want to live?"

Stephen considers carefully before he answers. "I don't think that is his strongest impulse right now."

This week, his family has finally traveled from the East Coast to see him. They hadn't come the last time; with a tinge of bitterness, Stephen told me they considered their son's near fatal illness an inconvenience. This visit, after they stopped briefly at the hospital to check in, they decided it was a good opportunity to go sightseeing.

It was after their first appearance in his hospital room that Dirk developed pneumonia.

Dirk remembers his adolescence as one of great rebellion, testing the values of an accomplished family headed by a high-powered executive. His father had only one expectation for his creative, artistic son: follow in his footsteps into the family business. When it became clear that would never happen, his father wrote him off.

Days before he became ill, Dirk had just completed shooting some lucrative work in commercials. And after years of struggling financially, he was in final negotiations for a major television development deal. It looked like real success was just before him. He had said to me, "I'm going to prove my family wrong."

As he lay in his hospital bed, breathing through a respirator, it is easy to see the little boy inside Dirk, still crying out for his parents' attention and love.

I've often wondered if those who have the ability to heal also have the converse ability to attract illness. Was Dirk willing to take his body to the brink of death to create a kind of final test to see if his parents really loved him?

I don't know. But it reminds me again that parental love is a powerful thing. I can't count the number of friends who, after years of therapy, have come to realize that the primary motivator in so many of their life choices is a subconscious yearning to earn the approval of their parents.

I see the eagerness in the eyes of our new sons when they show us something they've made. To know we think they are good and smart and wonderful means the world to them. And I see how quickly they shut down whenever something comes up that reminds them of their birth parents. The loss of their love affects the boys profoundly; they can only hint at the depth of their misery and pain.

As much as we love them, we cannot replace the parents who gave them life. All we can do, while raising them as our own, is try to give them tools to help them deal with their grief. I can't help but wonder if their loss inhibits them from fully receiving love from us; I wonder what kind of healing they will need to fully open their hearts again.

The circle of friends continues to hold Dirk in their prayers, and our boys pray that he will be healed, too. It's a task they take very seriously; somehow, without knowing the full story, they seem to understand the profundity of his need. As we pray, I visualize a genuine connection of love in his family; in that connection, I know, Dirk may find the miracle of life.

# Live from the Academy Awards

It's a gray Saturday morning in Los Angeles, following more than a week of torrential rain. Our neighborhood, nestled in the hills between Hollywood and the Valley, has been bound in by preparations for the Academy Awards, which take place tomorrow at the theater down the hill. Streets around us have been closed; the traffic, normally heavy, has slowed to a glacial stop. The entire hillside neighborhood, used to being trapped by the hoopla for the past four years, has packed in groceries and supplies in preparation for the siege.

Since Monday, helicopters have hovered over our house, starting in the predawn hours and staying throughout the day. Their only purpose is to provide breathless coverage about the erection of bleachers and the laying of red carpet. It's disconcerting to turn on the television and have the noise from the helicopter carrying the camera that provides the picture drown out the sound of awestruck reporters.

This year, at least, the concern over security is not as high as it was after 9/11—there are no police with Uzis posted at our corner. But even so, it's hard not to feel like this is an unwanted disruption in our lives; it takes twice as long to drive the boys back and forth to school each day because we must cross the red carpet barrier that now cuts us off from the rest of the city.

Tomorrow, the limousines carrying the luminaries will park on Highland Avenue and block the exit from our neighborhood; trucks and security will block the other exit at the end of our street, just behind the theater. And we will gather round the TV to watch what is happening on a nearby street where we normally walk our dogs, glad the week of inconvenience is nearly over.

From the window over my desk, I can look down the hillside and see the complex where the awards are given. My view is hampered by new growth among the ficus trees we planted two years ago. They provide a backdrop for the wonderful fountain that greets visitors as they climb the steps up to our home—but now I realize they also create one more welcome barrier between us and the hectic pace of life in Hollywood just below.

This year, the hoopla feels even more like an illusion. Since the boys came to us, finding time to see a "grown-up" film (those that don't feature Disney stars or animation) is a low priority; we've only seen two of the five films nominated for Best Picture. The boys are happily oblivious to the Oscar frenzy—their only real complaint is that the noise of the helicopters makes it difficult to concentrate when they are playing football in the driveway.

It's funny how my priorities changed when I became a father. Last year, we sat on a couch with Lorna Luft at a friend's party, roaring at her wicked comments about the parade of stars that couldn't hold a candle to her mother. It felt like we were in on one great big private joke, inside the most revered of all Hollywood circles.

This year, we are clearly on the outside; no invitations to coveted parties have come our way. Three children have meant immediate removal from some unforgiving guest lists. I'm aware of that in the same way I am aware of the constant drone of the helicopters overhead. It's a nuisance—but it has no real impact on my life.

We've invited some of the boys' friends and their families to come over and watch the awards, and the boys are excited to help me prepare food to feed everyone. They volunteer to mix the batter for brownies, sauté onions and garlic for the roast, and chop vegetables for salad. They even polish silver and roll napkins for the buffet table. It's not the Awards that excite them; it's the fact that we are entertaining as a family, and everyone has a part to play.

Stirring pasta sauce on the stove, I watch them as they hover over the kitchen counter, focused on their tasks. Every few seconds, they look up to show me what they've done. Their eagerness makes me smile. I used to hate sharing the kitchen when cooking big meals; today, I am aware of how happy it makes me to share mundane tasks with three eager helpers, and I know from their faces that they, too, are happy to share the work with me.

Decorating cupcakes with sprinkles and colored frosting is not, perhaps, how I once envisioned my life. But there is a calm richness to this experience I can't help but treasure—I wouldn't trade this for anything. Forty years ago, I learned to cook at my grandfather's knee, tugging at his pant leg to show me what he was doing. Now, I've been blessed with three boys who do the same.

Here in our little hillside aerie, tucked away from the Dream Factory below, I marvel at the two worlds that coexist in this corner of the globe. As much as I love to peer down into that other world, I am deeply grateful my feet are firmly planted in the world where helicopter noise and red carpets are just one more excuse for our family to celebrate together.

# Mr. Grumpy

My boys have started calling me "Mr. Grumpy," and a better nickname couldn't be found. Many days I wake up out of sorts, beleaguered by constant chores but too anal to let them sit while I take a few minutes to attend to my own needs. The months of self-neglect are getting to me. Typically, when the alarm goes off, I trudge downstairs, feed the dogs, empty the dishwasher, lay out the bowls and cereal and milk for the boys' breakfast, get their lunches ready, and fold the laundry from the last load the night before.

There are days when this ritual works for me; but there are far too many days when I feel like a resentful house drudge schlepping about in slippers and robe, fixated on mundane activity that is making my brain and spirit turn to mush. By the time I trudge back upstairs and sit at my desk for a brief interlude of quiet before everyone else wakes up and the house bursts into pandemonium, I am already far from center.

This is typically my only time alone each day, when quiet reigns and I can think without distraction. But it often feels like a Herculean effort to take advantage of the early morning stillness to focus and tune in. This is supposed to be my quiet time, those few graceful moments of Zen where I can connect to the universe and connect to my spirit— but I often find all I can do is make the "to do" list for the day, filled with a vague unease that I am missing the forest for the trees.

I don't think I am alone in this; almost everyone I know struggles to juggle the immediate demands of each day with their hunger to find spiritual nourishment in a parched world. It sometimes feels like we as humans are doubly plagued: we know enough to know there is something greater out there and long for it instinctively, but we are so finite and limited in our capacity that it is always feels just beyond our reach.

When I was younger and considered myself an evangelical Christian, I was taught to start my day with a devotional period called a "quiet time." It was supposed to include a few minutes of Scripture reading, a few minutes of quiet meditation, and a few minutes of intercessory prayer. Always a creature of habit, I rarely missed that time each morning, methodically marking the margins of my Bible with color-coded notes and slogging through my index cards filled with prayer requests and concerns.

But even then, I found meaning in the ritual itself, not in any significant connection to a higher power. Once I left my desk, the ritual was done. Rarely would anything from my "quiet time" impose itself on the rest of the day.

Today I'm struggling to find my center: I pray, I try to meditate, I try to consciously breathe and calm myself. But nothing seems to be working. I'd gotten up early to try to work a bit on a project with a tight deadline before the boys got up, but just as I am getting into it, I can hear Matthew's determined banging up the stairs. Every morning he pounds his foot into each tread as he comes up; it's his own little processional that proclaims, "I am here! Pay attention to me!" With the pounding echoing off the walls, I'm forced to bend to his will and do just that.

When the pounding stops, I look to the doorway. Matthew is standing there in his favorite blue dinosaur pajamas, lower lip quivering. "What's wrong, Matthew?"

It's the opening he is looking for. Rushing in, he flings his arms around my neck. "I asked Dereck to play with his new Gameboy game, and he wouldn't let me."

He sits in my lap and we talk, and Matthew begins to understand he can't expect to use Dereck's brand-new game right away. I tell him he has special permission to wrap up in a blanket on the couch and watch cartoons for a while, and he marches back downstairs, content. Tucked in with the Cartoon Network, he'll be occupied and content.

I turn back to my work and try to focus again. Before I know it, a sour-faced Dereck is standing next to me, his blond hair tangled and sticking out. "Matthew woke me up. He climbed up in my bunk bed and started shaking me, and now I can't go back to sleep." Now I know why the usually generous Dereck said no.

Dereck, too, wants to be cuddled and coaxed from his dark, still-sleepy mood. He's like me—once he's up, he can't go back to sleep. And like me, if he's not coaxed in just the right way, his irritability will hover about him like a cloud the rest of the day. I tickle and tease him, and Bruno, our new Bernese mountain dog puppy, brings us shoes and slippers he's collected from around the house. We laugh at the growing pile on the office floor, and Dereck's soon ready to head downstairs, a bit more cheerful. Now I can go back to work.

I decide I need to do something outside, to experience a bit of physical exertion and to breathe some fresh air. I go out to the back patio and begin to trim the potted rose bushes that Anthony gave us, knowing he'll be checking on them the next time he's over. Even that is interrupted; the gardener has come to trim the trees and clean up the back area, overgrown since the rains came a few weeks ago. I'd forgotten he was due today. The dogs hear his truck and start to bark and circle the door, in high gear at the invasion of their territory.

I sigh and know it's time to surrender; the real day for the household has begun, and any chance to work is gone until the boys have gone to bed.

I am irritable and angry, mad at the world that my moment of peace is fractured again. And so I remain, wielding my foul humor like a sword until my boys, teasing me in the very way I often try to tease them out of bad moods, call me "Mr. Grumpy." My spirits lift for a moment, but not for long; it's easier to stay in that grumpy space.

Later, I realize how much of the day I've spent being miserably angry. Before the boys say good night, we sit together and goof around, telling stories and being silly. Michael giggles and tells me I need to watch the movie *Anger Management*. Dereck guffaws, but eyes me warily to see how I will react.

I laugh with them; but underneath, I feel a twinge of despair, frustrated at my own weakness and inability to control my mood. Do I really want my kids to see me as a chronic anger machine?

"Help me," I pray again, as I kiss them goodnight.

I turn down the lights and sit in the near dark room, lost in thought and looking out the window into the cloudy night sky and the city lights below. The clouds are lit up from the wide expanse of city streets; they seem to converge in some distant spot, light and air mixed, fused into one.

Jesus said, "The Kingdom of God is within you," and for the first time, I realize there is a dual act of looking in and looking out that comes with prayer. A connection to God starts with the yearning for transformation, a willingness to acknowledge the dark spaces, to invite them to become flooded with light.

The transformation itself is as fluid as this night sky. For once, the opening is there, the light enters and fills and surrounds me, creating something entirely new and beautiful from those earthbound elements, fusing us and him into one.

I sit, watching the light and clouds mingle; I feel that mingling of light and dark in my own soul: gentle, slow, steady. Every dark place is not illuminated, I know, but perhaps a there is a bit more light now than earlier today. Suddenly, my anger lifts. I murmur a quiet thank-you and go off to join Michael, already asleep in our bed.

## Radio Days

I have a secret vice.

Every once in a while, as I'm driving in the afternoon, I like to listen to Dr. Laura. It's not that I agree with her advice; it's not that I value her bitch slapping; and I would never support any of the advertisers paying her to shill their products during her three-hour diatribe.

As a new parent who is trying to learn how to encourage my children to make good, healthy choices, I listen because her hectoring is the ultimate object lesson of what *not* to do.

I am ashamed to admit I can sometimes hear my own voice emanating through those thin, shriveled lips; I can cut, slice, dice, or shred with the same precision. As I listen, I actually feel the deflation of her callers, sudden converts to masochism who feebly murmur, "Yes, Dr. Laura" while being eviscerated for their troubles. And I think, *My God, do I sound like that when I talk to Michael, Dereck, or Matthew?*

My friends and family, when they dare, tease me about my blunt advice. There's not a one who has not been treated to a direct, spare-no-feelings tirade. I used to blame this peccadillo on being an oldest child; my job was to make my brothers and sister jump. But it's a skill that has long outlived its fraternal usefulness.

As my boys can attest, I've honed this skill to a science. Like a bloom of evening shade facing the morning sun, they close up faster than our new puppy can clean out his dog dish whenever I start in on them.

When six-year-old Matthew used the new guest towels I'd just set out in the bathroom to wipe poster paint off his face and hands minutes before dinner guests arrived, I sprang like a panther. Little red dots formed on his cheeks as I leaned over him, lecturing that he should have been paying attention—and what was he doing in the poster paint anyway? He didn't say a word, but when I finally turned on my heel and marched away, he fled to his bunk bed, burying tears in his pillow.

By the time I could chastise the boys for spilling cereal all over the floor before school and failing to clean it up, we were already rushed and in the car on the way to school; I ruminated most of the way, griping about traffic and their general sloppiness. Dereck, riding shotgun, turned and stared out the window, nostrils flaring. Finally, just a block away from school, he turned to me and said quietly, "I didn't spill the cereal. You shouldn't yell at me."

Of course, he was absolutely right. "Guilty as charged," I said, doing my best to apologize as they fled from the car into the schoolyard. As I drove home, I nearly knocked myself out banging my head on the steering wheel. What was I doing?

Later that week, our friend Jennifer sat at our kitchen counter, eating a sandwich while her kids and ours were playing outside. "It scares me how much my daughter is just like me," she said. "She emulates everything I do."

I shook my head, irritated again by the latest mess. "Sometimes I wonder if anything I say ever gets through to them."

Jennifer put down her sandwich, cocked her head slightly and raised one eyebrow. "Deee-rrrrr-eeeck," she said, a perfect imitation of me on a tear. Then she burst out laughing. "That's just me imitating him imitating you. He does it better than I do, you know."

A part of me was pleased Dereck could mimic my voice and gestures, but a bigger part of me was horrified. If my kids are sponges, just what are they absorbing from me?

I do get some clues. The first week they were in the house, they barged into the bathroom to watch me brush my teeth and then asked for a Sonicare toothbrush like mine. They'd never seen dental floss before; now they use it every day. They know the baristas at the Starbucks closest to our house, they love to watch the Food Network, and they even eat artichokes.

But it scares me to think about what else they learn when they watch me throw a temper tantrum or chew one of them out. I shudder to think they will turn out the same way: hyper-perfectionists with a sharp tongue and a low tolerance for disorder. I hate the thought that I might have already become one of those parents whose mantra is, "Do as I say, not as I do."

For the first few months, we had a rule in our house: any time the boys caught someone swearing, they would get a dollar (shades of *uber*-Catholic Loretta Young). With their hyper-vigilant hearing, they quickly supplemented their allowance mightily. If a driver did something stupid in front of us, the kids automatically turned to me expectantly, waiting for the inevitable expletive. I tried switching to Italian for a while, but they figured out which words were bad almost as soon as they popped out of my mouth. I rescinded the rule when I realized I would soon go broke.

The hardest thing about being a parent, I'm learning, is the difference between knowing what is right for your kids and doing it. Mind you, I'm really clear about what they need: love, support, and a consistent routine that makes them feel safe and secure. They don't need lectures (at least most of the time!), and they definitely don't need me turning into a shrew at the drop of hat.

And that's why I listen to Dr. Laura, especially as I'm on my way to pick up the boys from school. It's a way to clear my head and remind myself of my priorities. And, when I listen to my words coming out of her mouth, it's a good reminder of the person I don't want to be.

# The Freshman Twenty

My mom sends Valentines to each of the boys, and when they open them, they start jumping up and down. When I see the gift certificates from McDonald's, I groan. Now they have a good excuse to head for the Golden Arches and order Big Macs and fries, Chicken McNuggets, and Happy Meals.

"See, Daddy John, now you don't have to spend your money on food you don't like," says Dereck. But the problem is, I like it too much. And it's beginning to show.

Edy Garety, one of the psychologists we work with at UCLA, giggles when she tells us, "Most adoptive parents I've seen gain a lot of weight when the kids move in. They don't have enough time to exercise, and they wind up making foods kids like, which aren't always the healthiest."

I'm ready to retort, "Tell me about it," but I hold my tongue, and instead look at the burgeoning roll growing around my middle. It looks like those hot dogs that plump when you cook them. "At least I can still see my feet," I tell myself, but I wonder how long that will last. Thank God they're a size twelve. I should have a few more months before they are completely lost to my sight.

The boys, on the other hand, are skinny. And they stay skinny, no matter how much they eat. What they can burn off just by breathing sticks to my ribs like glue. And I have less self-control than they do.

Gone are the days when Michael and I ate healthy salads and chicken for dinner, with an occasional fat-free sorbet thrown in for dessert. Since the boys arrived, I've had more pizza, orange chicken, chili cheese fries, and stuffed burritos than any time since adolescence. And I can't turn my face away from any of it. Putting a French fry in front of me is like Pavlov ringing a bell. I ingest automatically.

These days, every time Michael goes to the store, he comes back with peanut butter cups and cookie dough ice cream. If that's not enough, whenever one of the boys says, "I want chocolate chip cookies," I haul out the mixing bowl and ingredients. In ten minutes flat, I've got a batch in the oven. We fight over who gets to lick the bowl, and we all stand in the kitchen waiting for the first tray to come out. For every one they eat, I help myself to two or three. I practically snort the crumbs.

With some horror, I realize I am turning into my great-grandmother. She lived with us briefly when I was a kid and would tell my mother that ten starving children in India could live on the food we kids left on our plates. But Great Grandma had known plenty of hard times and wasn't about to let all that good food go to waste. She'd sit at the dinner table after we'd run off to play and eat every leftover bite, complaining about waste all the while.

One night, as I'm spearing a chunk of burrito off Matthew's plate, I realize the apple didn't fall far from the tree. "I'm turning into Great Grandma," I wail when I call my mother.

"Just be glad you have a high metabolism," she says, unconcerned. In her mind, there's nothing to worry about. She used to make five pounds of pasta to feed five kids and never had leftovers. She still thinks of me as a lean, mean, eating machine.

When our friend Anthony, a retired anesthesiologist and one of our boys' "uncles," arrives early to go to the boys' school's fundraising auction, I'm ironing the shirt I plan to wear, irritated that I've waited until the last minute to do it. I'm so flustered I don't even notice I'm shirtless when he walks in. He gives me a once-over and a wry smile. "I know you think your stomach is sticking out. At least you look like you're doing a lot of sit-ups. I detect a six-pack underneath all that. Good for you." I glower at him and quickly cover myself up. I rush upstairs to finish dressing, but not before popping a little brownie into my mouth.

It's not that I don't exercise. That's the one thing I've managed to keep in my schedule each day; I head right to the gym the minute I drop the boys off at school. But thirty minutes on the treadmill don't compensate for a constant inhalation of donuts, cupcakes, and Tostitos. More drastic measures are in order.

I read books like *Outwit Your Weight* and bone up on Atkins and South Beach. I try to keep a food log, detailing every morsel I put in my mouth. I imagine what it would be like to have liposuction, but when a friend who has had it describes the body stocking you have to wear after, I picture myself as a stuffed sausage and say no.

It's only when I notice that Dereck lives to eat sugar that I actually start to pay attention to what's really going on. Given the choice between donuts or scrambled eggs and turkey sausage for breakfast, donuts win every time. If he packs his own lunch, it's filled with sugary snacks and little else; when I pick him up from school, he's often polishing off a fruit roll-up, one of the "healthy" snacks from the school's little store. When I ask him how many roll-ups he's eaten, he has to think a long while before he remembers. It's never less than three or four.

He's ingesting all this sugar unconsciously, and it has an enormous impact on his mood. He plays like a madman until he crashes, and then he gets grumpy and depressed. "Do you know what sugar does to you?" I ask him, and he shakes his head no. Together we start monitoring what he eats; the amount of sugar is staggering. At first, he refuses to believe he eats so much sugar—or that it could be bad for him.

So I begin to casually share information with him about nutrition and talk about the foods he needs to grow big and strong. He loves Brett Favre of the Green Bay Packers. "Hmmm," I say. "When Brett Favre is in training, do you think he eats a lot of gummy bears?"

Last night, as we were making lunches for school in the kitchen, Dereck says to me, "I only want to take healthy stuff today." I want to hug him, but I don't dare. Instead, I watch as he fills his lunchbox with turkey, some cheese, an apple, and an orange. "Why don't you take a few peanut butter pretzels, too?" I ask.

He thinks for a moment and says, "That should be okay," and loads them in.

It doesn't take a psychologist to figure out there are lots of unconscious reasons Dereck has learned to love sugar. But no ten-year-old, no matter how self-aware, is going to understand that when he reaches for candy, he is trying to compensate for feeling abandoned by his mother and trying to self-medicate.

What he does understand is that it gives him a momentary rush, but when he pays attention, he sees that he doesn't feel as good later on. "Sometimes I get a headache after I eat too much candy," he tells me. "And I don't like getting headaches." All I can do is help him make those connections and help him to see how better choices could help him avoid the things he doesn't want.

Of course, all this work with Dereck is rubbing off on me. I'm learning to be more conscious about what I'm putting into my mouth. I'm learning to figure out the triggers that make me compulsively suck down snacks. And like him, I may not completely understand all the reasons why; I can only work with what I know and make the best choices I can. It's all about being conscious, I know, but I expect

*John Sonego*

there will be other benefits as well. Someday soon, I just might be comfortable wearing a belt again.

## Our Ten-Year-Old Caretaker

It's a beautiful Saturday morning in Los Angeles. The sun is streaming in our windows, and the light plays lively on the hillside, still lush and green from all the rain this winter. Dereck, just out of the shower, comes and curls up in my lap, pressing his head against my shoulder.

"What's wrong, honey?" I ask.

"Nothing," he says, but his lower lip juts out a bit too much for me to believe him. He snuggles in, and his grip around my neck gets tighter.

We sit quietly for a moment, until I ask, "Are you thinking about your mom again?"

He nods, and slowly, a tear wells up in his eye.

In the last week, death has been an ever-present reality. On Monday, we found out that Mr. Tony, the kind, gentle older man who supervised the lunchroom and helped kids get into school in the mornings, died over the weekend of a heart attack. Our friend Rick's mother died of cancer on Friday, and an old friend of mine died of breast cancer just this morning. And the boys have watched the media coverage of the Terry Schiavo case and the death of Pope John Paul II. Suddenly, death is both immediate and all encompassing, and it marks their perception of their days visibly.

On Wednesday night, Daddy Michael and Dereck went to Lowe's to buy fencing material for the yard, and as they were loading the material on the roof of the van, a bungee cord snapped and created a big gash in the center of Michael's forehead. It bled profusely, and Dereck, the ten-year-old caretaker, had immediately taken charge.

Calmly, he'd walked Michael back into the store restroom, helped him clean the cut and held the compress until the bleeding stopped. "Can you drive home okay, Daddy Michael?" he asked. They drove home slowly, and the entire time Dereck kept up a cheerful patter, all the while watching Michael with a quiet vigilance to make sure he was all right.

When they got home, I took one look at the cut and said, "You'll need stitches. We've got to go to the emergency room." We called Uncle Anthony to stay at the house, and he was there in minutes. As soon as the adults took over, Dereck collapsed, shaking and crying. He'd been a trooper when he was needed, but now he could be a kid again. Breaking down, he sobbed, "You're not going to die, Daddy Michael, are you?"

"Of course not. The stitches will just help the cut heal better so I won't have a big scar. It doesn't hurt at all." When we left, Dereck was sitting in Anthony's lap, drying his eyes. Anthony, who loves to teach and expound on what he knows, was telling him all about the different ways a doctor might choose to treat the wound. Even through his tears, I could see the glazed look in Dereck's eyes. Anthony, who couldn't stop himself from teaching medicine, was imparting too much information to a boy whose mind was already on overload.

We didn't get back until well past midnight; Dereck was still awake, staring at the ceiling over his bunk. Only after his newly stitched dad checked in could Dereck finally relax enough to go to sleep.

Whenever scary things happen, Dereck immediately thinks about his mom. This week, he's mentioned her three different times, more than he has in the past six months. He even told Michael that he couldn't remember what she looked like anymore, and he wanted a picture so he wouldn't forget again.

When he climbs into my lap instead of running to play football outside this Saturday morning, I know he was thinking of her again. "Are you worried about how she is doing?"

He nods, and his lower lip begins to quiver. Though he could never say so, he knows she is at great risk because of her drug use and because her current boyfriend beats her. Whenever Dereck lets himself think about her, he is filled with dread.

"I have an idea," I say. "You're such a good writer. Why don't you write her a letter and tell her about everything you've been doing? You can send her a picture of you on the boogie board in Hawaii and maybe some other pictures, too."

He thinks for a moment, and then begins to get up. "I'll write it on my computer. Will you help me pick some pictures?" Before I can nod yes he is already gone. I've given him an easy way to deal with his feelings, a way that helps him feel like he has some control over what is going on.

While I clean up breakfast in the kitchen, he is up and down the stairs a couple of times with questions, until he runs back to say, "I'm finished. Come look."

He's written this letter to his mom, whom he hasn't seen now for nearly nine months:

> *Dear Mom,*
> *I hope you are happy where you are. We got a new dog named Bruno and he is a really sweet BERNESE Mountain DOG.*
> *I have been thinking about you a lot and I miss you very, very much. My brothers miss you and they love you too. Daddy John and Daddy Michael are very good parents. We had been doing a lot of things with them. We went to Hawaii, Florida, Michigan, Palm Springs, and Big Bear.*
> *Can you send me a picture of you and write back?*
> *Love Dereck Arden Sonego*

I print out the letter, and he signs it in his new cursive signature. For more than an hour, we cull through all the pictures from our trips, his school play, and the awards ceremony where he received a football trophy. We put together a package of his favorite shots. On the back of each, we write a brief description so his mom will know what's been going on.

I tell Dereck we'll forward the letter to Christina, the social worker who has her address, and ask Christina to mail it for us. His mom can write back through her if she wants. He stands over my shoulder as I write the envelope and put the package together.

Once it's done, he smiles, freed from his misery, "Can we invite Giacomo over for a play date today?"

Giacomo, one of his best friends from school, stays the night, and they are up late playing games on PlayStation and watching videos of *The Family Guy*. The next morning, we all go to the memorial service for Mr. Tony at the boys' school.

When two of the boys' teachers stand up to sing, the four boys, sitting in a long row, sit up and pay rapt attention. Ms. Tina and Mr. Ray sing sweetly and powerfully, their voices blending in a complicated, delicate harmony they must have worked long hours to create. After, as some of their classmates get up to share memories of Mr. Tony, all of the boys seem surprised. Little Michael whispers, "I'd be too afraid to go up on the stage." Even Matthew, usually fidgety, sits in solemn stillness; Mr. Tony would say "Give me five!" to him every morning as I dropped them off.

Throughout the ceremony, Dereck looks over at me, tears spilling onto flushed cheeks. I know he's thinking about Mr. Tony. But from the look in his eyes, I know he is also thinking about the mom who is never far from his thoughts, a mother he loves and knows he may never see again. I reach across the other boys to squeeze his shoulder, my own eyes a little wet.

# Trade in the Tang and Song Dynasties

It's 5:30 on a warm Friday morning, and I'm sitting at my desk, proofreading a report about trade in the Tang and Song Dynasties for the fifth time. Little Michael has to turn it in three hours from now. Glassy-eyed, I'm irritable and frustrated, and as my red pen flies petulantly across the pages, I feel like a cranky newspaper editor.

This project has been four weeks in the making, at least according to the schedule created by his social studies teacher, Ms. Laira. Their class has been studying China, and Michael and two of classmates had selected this topic because they thought it was cool that the Chinese invented gunpowder and matches. They were disappointed to learn later the Chinese had just appropriated gunpowder from the Arabs, but their joy returned when they learned the Chinese had figured out how to attach it to arrows to create the first incendiary bombs.

Last Saturday, the boys met at our house and spent the afternoon alternating between taking turns at PlayStation, playing with Michael's hamsters, and writing the introductory paragraph. Ms. Laira's a smart woman—she had them turn in the introduction and an outline for her approval the Monday before the paper was due. Used to working with procrastinating seventh graders, she's given them specific milestones along the way so they aren't pulling their first all-nighter just before the paper is due.

After nearly five hours and two dozen chocolate cookies (the chunkier of the two classmates eats a dozen on his own), they bring the introduction to me to read. While I sit at my desk chair, they sit on the floor, playing with the dogs that are following them everywhere, pushing and shoving and giggling. They at the awkward stage where their voices are changing, and the air is filled with squeaks and squawks and ear-shattering four-octave glissandos. Between the dogs and the boys, the room sounds like a tone-deaf church choir, with everyone warming up at once.

Michael keeps his eye on me as I read. When I look up, he quiets down the other boys. "My dad's almost as hard as Ms. Laira," he says proudly, setting me up perfectly.

"So boys, what's the purpose of an introductory paragraph?" I say, relishing my self-assumed role as their new instructor.

We spend the next thirty minutes in an impromptu question-and-answer session, culminating with them clustered around the computer while I retype and reshape the introduction, all of them throwing out ideas and comments. When it's done, they run clacking and screeching down the stairs, back to PlayStation and the remaining cookie crumbs.

Daddy Michael, who has been listening in the other room, comes into the office. "You shouldn't write their paper for them," he says.

"I'm not!" I protest. "I just tried to help them get focused. If they get the introductory paragraph down, writing the rest of the paper will be a snap."

One glance at the manic look in my eyes and he walks away. This isn't a battle he needs to take on.

"Damn," I think. "He knows me too well."

Ms. Laira gives them time to write the paper during class, but she's also sent an e-mail to parents to alert them that the boys should be doing some work on the project at home. On Monday, Tuesday, and Wednesday nights, I press Michael to write. Every night, he tells me Josh is doing this, or Giorgio is doing that—he insists he's already done what he needs to do to contribute to the team effort. I have a foreshadowing of what our Thursday evening will be.

On Thursday, I come home from a late afternoon meeting, after Michael has picked up the boys at school. Before I can put my backpack down, they start circling me, thrusting math problems and reading journals and science questions at me, saying, "Check this!" and "I need help with … " and "I can't figure out …"

I close my eyes for a brief moment and try to breathe. There's dinner to be made, I've got a deadline to meet, and I've got to finish the agenda for the all-day meeting I have tomorrow. "Okay, okay, boysenberries, one at a time."

I finish with Dereck and Matthew quickly. All the while, Michael paces anxiously, chewing on his cuticles. I know exactly what's coming.

He whines, "I don't know how to type the bibliography. Will you do it for me?"

"You've had all week to do this project. Why are you waiting until the last minute?"

"I'm not," he sputters, launching into a litany of excuses about all the things Giorgio and Josh failed to do.

Irritated, I cut him off. "Michael, this paper is your responsibility. I'm not going to do it for you. You can type the bibliography. I don't have time."

"But I don't know how!" he wails.

"Follow the format Ms. Laira gave you! I'll be happy to check it. But I'm not about to type it."

"Fine!" He stomps off to his room. If he hadn't already messed up his door so it jams a bit, he would have slammed it.

As I start dinner, the phone rings. I hear a bit of breathing and a few cracks and squeaks before I can make out, "Uh, uh, this is Giorgio. Is Michael there?" Two minutes later, the phone rings again, and it's Josh. In the half hour I prepare dinner, they call at least ten times. Finally, I tell Michael to take the phone into his room, even though I'm afraid it will disappear forever under the piles of clothes and papers and candy wrappers he navigates every night to find his bed.

After dinner, Michael brings me a draft of the paper and confesses that he's supposed to write the last section as well as complete the bibliography. "I don't know what to say," he tells me, the fear in his face palpable.

Throughout the night, between phone calls and e-mails from his cohorts containing copy Michael must cut and paste, his anxiety level goes through the roof, and I begin to feel pity for my struggling son.

Against my will, I'm sucked into the vortex of this abysmal project. I start to hate the Chinese and begin contemplating how I can get even with Ms. Laira. By 10:30, any hope of completing my own work gone, so I climb into bed, weary and worried. How is he going to pull it off?

Just before I turn out the lights, he brings in draft number five and drops it on the bed. "Michael, I just can't read this again tonight," I tell him.

"But you've got to!"

"I'll get up early to read it, and I'll wake you up early so you can finish it. Okay?"

He whines, "You mean I have to get up early?"

"If you want the damned thing done, you'd better," I snap, and turn off the light.

When the alarm goes off at 5:15, Daddy Michael, restless beside me, mutters, "Don't write his paper for him."

"I won't," I promise, and head downstairs to make coffee.

Coffee in hand, I stick my head into Michael's room and see his long, skinny feet poking out from his covers. The room smells like hamster poop. "Oh, let him sleep," I say, and trudge upstairs.

I spend the next hour and half reworking the paper, adding facts, creating summaries for each section, and massaging phrases. I know what the boys are trying to say, but they just couldn't get there. Every few minutes, Michael calls out from the bedroom, "Don't write his paper for him!"

"I'm not," I respond, and turn back to my work.

By seven, it's whipped into credible shape, and I go down to wake up Little Michael. "Michael, time to get up. You need to read your paper so you know what you're saying."

"Huh?" he mutters. Half an hour later, we sit at the desk, going over the final version I've just printed out. He barely glances through it before reaching for the stapler.

"Thanks, Dad," he says, as he stuffs it into his backpack.

It's only when I'm driving to the meeting I'm unprepared to lead that I start to beat myself up about being Michael's enabler. Why didn't I follow through on making him take responsibility for himself? What kind of miserable parent am I, that I could let myself do such a thing? What did he really learn from this project except that he could manipulate me into taking care of things for him?

I'm tempted to call Daddy Michael to share when suddenly something else occurs to me. The paper Little Michael turned in is still missing its bibliography.

I start to laugh, and flying down the freeway, I vow to myself I'll never write a paper for him again.

# The Throne Room

In a hectic home, you've got to carve out an oasis of privacy. My mom locks her studio to keep prying eyes away. One of my brothers won't allow anyone into his workshop in the garage; another has a huge walk-in closet even his girlfriend can't enter.

My oasis used to be my bathroom.

It's not big. In fact, it's probably the smallest space in the house, built into an oddly angled space in the guest bedroom. With no windows and walls so close I can stand and touch any of them from the center of the space, it is dark and cramped, even a bit dingy. When I moved in and claimed it as my own, there was a sink, a toilet, and a small shower. We added a teeny cabinet for toiletries, towels, and some books, and I hung some art on the tiny walls to perk it up.

Michael said to me, "I don't understand why you won't use the master bath. It's more than twice the size."

"Because the master bath doesn't have doors, and I can't poop feeling like I'm sitting out in the open," I replied. "I need to be able to close the door."

In a house designed around big, open spaces and lots of windows and light, my dark little bathroom became a sanctuary. Often, I'd lock the door just to read and have a moment of quiet, shutting out the dogs and the television and the phone.

That is, until the boys moved in. Moments after I sat on the toilet right after their arrival, there was a knock on the door. "Daddy John, where should I put my Power Rangers?"

I thought, *We need to set some rules here*, as I opened the door a crack, and Matthew pushed his way in.

The next morning, it was Dereck who pushed open the door. "Daddy John, what's that string you use between your teeth?"

Within seconds, all three boys were rifling through the drawers and opening the medicine cabinet, examining my razor and deodorant and toothpaste.

"Why do you use that kind of soap?"

"Why do you shave your neck going up instead of down?"

"Why do you use that kind of deodorant?"

At first, their interest in my hygiene habits was gratifying. "So this is what being a dad is supposed to be like," I thought. "You get to teach them things they'll use their entire lives."

But pretty soon I got tired of them pushing open the door every time I tried to pee. "Guys, you need to learn to knock if the bathroom door is closed."

"Okay, okay," they said. But I learned to brace myself when standing at the toilet so I wouldn't topple over every time the door swung open. It was like they were clairvoyant. The minute the door closed, they'd find some reason to push their way in.

Soon, they decided they preferred my bathroom to their own. Crusty yellow stains grew along the base of the bowl on the granite floor. Toothpaste spittle with bits of chocolate and cookie clung to the sink. The steady drip, drip, drip of a faucet that was never completely shut off started to wear a groove into the shower pan. Every morning, I'd have to scrub the toilet just to feel comfortable using it.

Once the boys started using my bathroom, it was open season for Daddy Michael, too. His favorite trick was to use all the toilet paper and leave the empty roll on the holder. My poor quiet little sanctuary fairly cried from the overuse and abuse.

It was enough to unhinge me. "Stay out of my bathroom!" I'd scream.

"Okay, okay," they all said. But they kept on coming.

My mom used to say the secret of her near fifty-year marriage to my father was the fact that they never shared a bathroom. Her bathroom was sacrosanct; as kids, we never dared to enter, even though we always wondered what she did in there for two hours every morning.

Sometimes, she'd open the door and we'd have a clue. Clouds of steam, carrying wafts of perfume, make-up, and cigarettes, would billow out like smoke signals. It would drive my father crazy, especially when we were waiting for her to finish so we could leave to go somewhere.

"Go tell your mother to hurry up," he'd say to us kids.

"Not me," we'd each answer. We knew what would happen if we dared knock on that door. "Maybe you should go."

Dad would just shake his head and continue pacing. He knew better, too.

To this day, none of us will use her bathroom. How did my mother do it?

She giggled when I asked her. "I just made you afraid. But I never did anything. I didn't have to."

I remembered that. We wouldn't dare bother her.

"With five kids, bathroom time was my lifeline to sanity. So I just locked the door. And I wouldn't open it unless the house was on fire."

"That's it? You just locked the door?"

"Yes. There's no reason they need to come in there unless you want them to. Set some limits. Show some backbone. Make 'em afraid. If you want your privacy, that's what you have to do."

The next morning, I locked the door with a big ceremonial click. Within seconds, the handle turned. And turned again, and again, and again. When that didn't work, they tried knocking on the door. Soon, the walls were reverberating with the pounding. I reached out to steady the picture tilting dangerously above the light switch, and then turned on the fan to muffle the noise.

In a few minutes, I emerged, teeth brushed and face shaved. The boys were gathered around the door, bedeviled and grimacing. "Ready to go to school?" I said with a smile.

As we loaded backpacks and lunchboxes into the car, I smiled again. "The next time someone pounds on my bathroom door, it had better be an emergency."

Over the next week, the bathroom interruptions slowly tapered off. Once they figured out they would never get in there again, they gradually gave up trying. Now I can read and primp and shut out the world. Those few minutes I claim for myself are exactly as mom described—a small lifeline to sanity.

I come out with my brow unfurled and my spine stiffened, ready to take on the next challenge. Except, of course, on days I reach for the toilet paper and find nothing but a little cardboard circle on the holder.

# No Birthday Bubbles in Texas

Twenty kids are screaming and jumping into the pool on a gorgeous sunny afternoon. Suddenly, from the second floor balcony overlooking the water, a bubble machine pumps out cascades of bubbles. They gleam in the sunlight as they slowly fall onto the heads of the kids bobbing in the water below. When the kids stop and stare up in wonder, all the parents surrounding the pool stop, too. We're all caught up in a magical moment, a gorgeous Hollywood display we all know is special.

But since this is Hollywood, that moment is fleeting. As the bubbles pop when they hit the water, the kids start to splash and scream again, with an expectant air that something new and just as special will come to them in the next few minutes. The parents go back to their margaritas and diet sodas and conversation, a lingering thought in all of our heads: "How am I going to top *this* for *my* kid's birthday?"

Matthew's best friend Jason, his classmate in first grade, is turning seven. His two dads, who adopted him as a baby from Guatemala, have invited all of Jason's classmates, their parents, and his teachers over for the afternoon.

Matthew's class has twenty-one kids, and they are a wonderfully diverse bunch. Seven children are adopted; three have a pair of dads for parents. A few others have a single mom or dad. Many of the children are mixed race, and every color and every continent is represented. There is something extraordinarily beautiful, watching all of them play together in the pool.

Jeff and Wade are gracious hosts. The kids are well tended; there's a lifeguard and an attendant to watch them in the jumper, and tables of healthy and not-so healthy snacks are scattered around the well-groomed yard. For us parents, they've provided huge pitchers of margaritas, beer, wine, and sodas—and the dining room, which opens onto the pool and patio area, is filled with indulgent finger food only the adults will enjoy.

It's easy to settle into comfortable chairs, with an eye on Matthew splashing, and chat with people we really like.

Lina's mom is from Switzerland, and on her last trip home to Bern, she bought us the traditional dog collar for our new Bernese mountain dog puppy. She's a hoot, and today she encourages us to make sure Matthew learns to hike in the hills around our home. "My father used to make us hike with him every weekend, and I always cried and hated it," she says. "But look at my legs now!" She gamely thrusts up one well-shaped, muscular leg, "Hard as a rock and no cellulite, even after a kid!"

Joe and Lauren, Sam's adopted parents, join us. They have also been fostering a beautiful baby girl, and they've just found out that the court will allow them to proceed with the adoption. Lauren gets a bit teary-eyed as she tells us the news, as baby Sadie leans toward me, wanting to play with the dragon design on my T-shirt. Sadie is soon sitting on my shoulders and we're walking around the pool, watching the kids. She burbles and pulls at my ears to tell me where she wants to go.

When we come back to our table, Riley's mom and dad, transplants from Canada, lean in conspiratorially. After Riley's dad nods an okay, his mom says to us, "I have an older sister I've never met. My parents had her when they were fifteen, and they gave her up for adoption. They finally told me about her a couple of years ago; until then, I thought I was an only child. I tried placing ads and doing a search. But I never found her. Maybe she's not interested. Or maybe she just never learned she was adopted." She looks over at the pool and says quietly, "I just want to see what she looks like."

Riley's dad reaches over and squeezes his wife's hand. "We think it's wonderful you kept the boys together. They'll always have their brothers in their lives."

Logan's mom, Robin, who hails from Philadelphia's Main Line and calls herself a reformed actress, cracks, "Yeah, yeah. We know all you gay dads are saints. But I have to tell you, every time Logan doesn't want to listen to me, he says, 'You're a mean mom. I want two fun dads like Matthew.' I haven't figured out a comeback to that one!"

Everyone around the table laughs, and all the gay dads bask in the sweet-natured support.

But as the kids play and the parents laugh, I can't help but think about what's happened this week in a state that's not so far away. On CNN this morning, I saw a story about a new bill that passed in the Texas legislature that bans gay foster parents from adopting the children they care for. The bill's sponsor, an old white sourpuss whose sense of misguided entitlement oozes out of every pore, told the interviewer, "Those gay people ain't fit to be parents."

I look at Matthew, Jason, Eduardo, and the other children in that pool who found safety and trust and love in the homes of gay men and women. And I suddenly shudder with vulnerability, horrified that those families—and my family—could be ripped apart in an instant if such a law were passed here.

I think back to just a few months ago to the boys' first night in the house after they moved in. I remember feeling overwhelmed and not sure what to do next, wondering if I had what it took to be a good father, whether I would know how to handle situations as they came up, whether I would be up to the challenge.

But with three expectant boys looking to you, you have no choice but to jump right in. We experience challenges every day, and somewhere along the line, something in me changed. I can't pinpoint the moment when it happened, or even how. All I know is that somehow, at some point, those boys became my own children. I love them deeply, totally, fully, like I have never loved anyone or anything in my life. And without me ever having to say it, I know they know it, and they trust in that truth like it's bedrock.

Matthew comes running up to me. "Daddy John, can I have some pizza now?"

I want to hug him and squeeze him as hard as I can, but I just say, "Of course you can, honey."

He scampers off to the pizza table and brings it back over to sit in my lap while he eats. He lifts his piece of pizza up toward me, saying, "Want some?"

I take a little bite and thank him. He sits there, munching contently, until he looks up at me again and asks, "Can we have birthday bubbles on my birthday, too?"

"Of course you can," I say again. I hug him before he runs off to play again, thinking how sad it is there will be no birthday bubbles in Texas this year.

## Telling Matthew

Driving home from dinner at a Chinese restaurant in the Valley, all three boys are giggling when the oldies station begins to play *Wild Thing*.

They all start singing at the top of their lungs:

*Wild thing, you make my heart sing,*
*You make everything groovy!*

I laugh. "How do you know this song?"

Little Michael answers, "It was my mom's favorite song."

They all grow quiet for a moment, thinking again about the woman they haven't seen in nearly a year.

Finally, Matthew speaks. "I don't understand why I'm not with my mom."

"We can talk about that, honey, when we get home."

"Okay." We drive the few remaining miles home in silence, the boys locked in their own thoughts.

It's the first time Matthew has ever said anything about being with his mother. We had wondered if he was too young to remember her, or if he was unconsciously blocking out memories.

After Matthew showers, he climbs into bed, and I sit down next to him. We'd gotten into the habit of saying a prayer together every night since his hamster, Blacky, died a few weeks before. Matthew was having bad dreams about Blacky and would wake up, upset and disturbed. Since we'd begun praying, he hadn't any bad dreams. Mentioning Blacky was often code for acknowledging he was feeling sad.

Just the night before, I had said to him, "Matthew, sometimes when you are feeling sad about Blacky, do you think you are feeling sad about other things, too?" He'd nodded yes.

"Do you know what else might make you sad?" He'd shaken his head no, and I gave him a hug.

"It's okay to recognize when other things might make you sad. When you can figure out what it is and talk about it, it is a way to help you feel better," I'd told him.

So tonight, when he looks up at me from his pillow, I know what he's been feeling. "Matthew, have you been thinking about your mom lately?"

He nods yes, his eyes wide. "When you've said that you miss Blacky, do you think maybe you were missing your mom, too?"

He nods again. His eyes began to fill with tears as he chokes out, "But that doesn't mean I don't love you and Daddy Michael!"

Now I understand. "Honey, I know you love me and Daddy Michael. And I know you love your mom. And it's good that you love your mom, because I know how much she loves you."

"But I don't know why we can't be with her."

"I can tell you why, if you want."

He nods again.

"Your mom loves you very much, but she isn't able to take care of you."

He nods.

"Matthew, you know that your mom had a problem with drugs, and that made it hard for her to take care of you. That doesn't mean she doesn't love you. It's just that when someone takes drugs like your mom, she's not able to take of her kids, no matter how much she loves them. I know that Carolina talked with all of you while you lived with Anna and David and explained that to you."

He begins to shake his head back and forth. "No, no. The neighbor put the drugs in my mom's front yard. That's why the police took her away."

"Matthew, I don't know if that's true or not. But when you were living with Anna and David, the judge wanted to give your mom another chance to show she could take care of you. So he ordered your mom to get drug tests every week, so they could tell if she was doing drugs or not. Do you know what a drug test is?"

He shakes his head no.

"A drug test shows whether or not you've been taking drugs. When they do a drug test, you have to provide a sample of your urine, and a doctor will test it for drugs. So every week, you mom would go to the doctor's office and she'd have to pee in a little cup, and the doctor would analyze it."

Matthew's little pug nose wrinkles in disgust. "That's gross."

"I know. But when you pee, that's one of your body's way of getting rid of something it doesn't need. So if you take drugs, it shows up in your urine. Your mom was tested once a week for nearly two years. And every time it was tested, it showed she was still using drugs. So the judge decided you should live with a family that loves you and would be able to take care of you. And so we were lucky enough to be able to adopt you."

He looks up at me, tears still in his round blue eyes, listening. "And so now you have a mom who loves you, and you have two dads who love you. And we get to take care of you."

"I know." He reaches up and puts his hand on the side of my head. He likes to rub the stubble; it makes him giggle.

"Do you worry about your mom sometimes?"

He nods yes. "Can we pray for her when we pray for our family?"

"Of course we can. What should we ask God for?"

"That he takes care of my mom and watches out for her."

"That's a good thing to pray for."

And so we pray for his mom that night. Then I sit with Matthew, stroking his head until he falls asleep. Abandonment can feel like a vast, immense cavern, but we have just turned on a light. We will work our way through.

# Part II

## Surfing the Learning Curve

Boys will be boys—and so will a lot of middle-aged men.
—*Kim Hubbard*

Everyone told us that having kids would change our lives. And indeed it did, in ways we did not expect. Learning to throw a football at age forty-six, learning the difference between an Xbox and PlayStation, and figuring out how to assemble a Bionicle were just a few of the unexpected lessons of our second year together.

But the biggest lesson of all was discovering that Daddy Michael and I are just little boys as well, only in larger, more wrinkled bodies, capable of the same tantrums and petulance that are the badges of honor for any preteen—our tantrums are just not as pretty.

## Peeing in a Cup

The boys are unsettled and unhappy, sitting in the pediatrician's front office. Waiting for their physicals and immunizations, the mood in the waiting room is tense. It's crowded and loud, filled with crying children, and no amount of comfort or shushing can settle some of them down. I watch the nurse behind the desk adjust her earplugs, pushing them deeper into her ears.

Our boys try to put on brave faces, but the noise and fear gets to them. Michael gnaws on his cuticles; Dereck chews on his lower lip; Matthew sits rigid, staring with saucer eyes at the tears and shrieks around him. When their turn comes, they march like little soldiers in the exam room, tense and tight.

Matthew screams and sobs when the needles poke him. Dereck, determined to be stoic, just clenches his jaw. But soon the pain is too much for him too, and he's crying and sniffling next to his brother. They cuddle in my arms, shaking, their tears creating big wet spots on my shirt. Little Michael affects the blasé nonchalance of a teenager, until he thinks I'm not looking; then, out of the corner of my eye, I watch his face contort in pain. I reach over to squeeze his hand, and he hangs on tightly.

No matter how much I try to tell them these shots will protect them from things that are far worse, this is the last place in the world they want to be. But when the doctor tells them he needs a urine sample and they must each pee in a cup, Dereck suddenly brightens. "Am I going to get paid for it? I used to make money peeing in a cup for my mom's friends," he says.

Michael tries to shut him up, whispering, "Don't say that." He knows why Dereck's urine was worth a couple of bucks. "You're not getting money for it today."

But Dereck, who loves any opportunity to earn money, won't stop. "Why not? Remember, I did it every week!"

Michael shakes his head again, a warning look on his face. He doesn't like to talk about their life before. His face flushes with shame, a blush of red spreading across his freckles.

"It's okay, Michael," I say. "Dereck, the doctor needs to run some tests, and there's no money involved here. I'm sorry."

Dereck looks crestfallen, and Michael turns away. When he looks back, our eyes meet; he knows that I now know one more shameful family secret. I nod at him, trying to tell him it really is okay. In his eyes, I see the grief of an older brother who is guilty he couldn't protect Dereck from such a terrible thing.

But the emotion doesn't last long; slowly, his face grows impassive, and his eyes become distant and unfocused. He's checked out, once again, until he can lock away the memories.

He tries so hard to contain his past. There are entire days when Michael is like this: going through the motions, vacant, shut down. He tries to make himself small, even invisible. I can sometimes smell his fear.

He can't let himself be alone, but he's too troubled to engage. He holds himself on the edge of family activity, a hunch-shouldered blank, immobile and passive. These are the times when I have to call his name three or four times before he answers, slowly and softly, as if his voice is coming through a fog.

Of all the boys, Michael has seen the most, and the ghosts he carries sometimes surround him like a shroud. He does his best to keep it all contained, but I know there will come a time when his memories will burst out, twisting and taunting him like a rag doll in the wind.

Buried secrets never die. They lie in wait, ready to create a fresh hell in already tormented hearts.

As the man who has only been his father for a year, I sometimes lie awake, asking myself, "What can I teach him?" I wonder at the karmic destiny that brought us into each other's lives. I see in him a mirror of myself at his age, wounded, lost, believing the only way to survive was to tamp down my own pain and try to lock it away.

I remember myself at fourteen, hiding behind the living room couch, stretched out as flat as I could, trying my best make myself invisible. Would it help him to know that when I was his age, I lived in agonizing self-doubt, that I chewed my fingernails with the same fervor as he, that I kept my hair long and in my eyes, just like he does, as a way to keep the world away?

I know, of course, the answer is no. Perhaps my stories may one day help illuminate my son's path—but he's not ready yet. His pain is too immediate, his wounds too fresh.

But in my mind's eye, I see the boy I once was, the long, lank hair that used to cover my head. I start to giggle, remembering how I much I fussed to straighten out its waves so it would hang precisely over my eyes. Back then, if someone had told me I'd be as bald as my father, I would have wanted to shoot myself on the spot.

Laughing at the memory, I bless the awkward skinny boy I once was. Self-absorbed as only a teenager can be, I saw my life before me as a long and painful road; now I realize it is a wide and perfect circle. That boy who once feared he was unlovable is blessed to love a child who feels the same. There's healing in that circle, knowing that what was once misery was nothing more than preparation for the greatest joy of my life.

And that's one of the great mysteries of life. Grace almost always works in the shadows, winnowing its way into those dark corners of shame or guilt. Grace is a gift of light, and within it are the very seeds of transformation. In a flash, they take root, and from ugliness grows beauty. It happened for me; and I know it will happen for my son.

## Family Secrets

As I walk up the aisle to the lectern to give my grandmother's eulogy, my mother grabs my hand and pulls me down to her. "Just don't make me cry," she whispers.

I nod and walk up to face the family and friends who have gathered to say farewell to my ninety-year-old grandmother, lying in the closed casket just in front of the lectern. The pastor, found by my cousin Sharon, has just finished a long Southern Baptist sermon about Miss Hattie coming to rest in Jesus. It had nothing to do with my grandmother's life. I'd watched my mother and her sisters twitch and twist during the sermon, knowing their mother would have said it was all a crock.

My aunts had come to me the moment I arrived, asking if I would speak. "She always thought you were smart," they coaxed. Somehow, I knew they would ask, and I'd spent the long flight to Tennessee making notes and remembering.

Mom sits on the edge of her seat at the end of the pew as I speak, her face immobile in grief. "Tears should be shed in private," she'd said earlier that day. My father, sitting next to her, once shared her reserve, but he's changed as he got older. He looks up at me, tears streaming down his cheeks. I try not to look at him—even though his head and shoulders are in my direct line of sight just over the casket—because it makes me choke up.

After the funeral, we bury Grandma in the small family cemetery on a hilltop surrounded by the Smoky Mountains she loved, a huge oak tree shading her grave, the graves of her parents, and the child she'd lost when she was very young. The sisters stay behind after everyone has left, for a few moments of private time.

Later, the family cars slowly wind their way through the hills and park on cousin Reba's property. Some of us decide to walk the mile back into the holler, to what was once my great-great-grandfather's property, down a long rough path and across a creek, far from the main road that led to town. I hadn't been there since we visited when I was seven.

Mom stays on Reba's porch, but my aunts borrow walking sticks, and we set out. The path is rocky through the trees, and the creek crossing is a challenge for them. There had once been a footbridge, they remember, but it is long gone. Aunt Elaine, the oldest, rolls up her slacks and says, "It's been fifty years since I've been here. If I've gotten this far, I'm not stopping now," and through the water she goes.

We come to a clearing where a small building—nothing more than a shack—is falling over itself, trees and brush already growing around and through it. It had once had two little rooms, one upstairs and one below, and a small porch. There'd been a fireplace to heat the house; you could see the remains of the stone in one corner. My great-grandmother had been the last one to live in the holler full-time, the one my mother and her sisters called "Maw." She'd died when she was 104.

"We used to walk down that little path to the spring to get our water," Aunt Jean Ann says, "and the outhouse was over there." One of her sons grabs a stick and pulls out some of the newspapers that had insulated the walls in the upper room. They are more than fifty years old, but the subscription labels are still readable.

"Oh my God. My Uncle Luther must have had these delivered here. He used to come here to write stories. He was a hermit. He'd disappear back here for months and nobody would see him. He'd come out with a bunch of stories he'd sell to *Modern Romance* magazine. That's how he made his living."

There is one sturdy poplar in front of the shack. Aunt Elaine touches it, smiling. "My grandfather planted this the day I was born. It's seventy years old." I take pictures of her and her children in front of it, their arms wrapped around each other.

As we made our way back, I ask my Aunt Jean Ann to tell me about what it was like visiting there when she was a kid. "Oh, we lived here with Maw for a year and a half once," she says. "Aunt Joy and I walked this path to get to school every day. But don't tell your mother I told you."

"Why did you live here?"

"It was one of the times when my parents weren't getting along. So Daddy sent Mom and the younger kids down here. Elaine was already married. Your mom was a senior in high school, and she refused to go, so she stayed in Cleveland with our father. Mom never stuck around here, and we never knew where she was off to. She'd disappear for weeks at a time." She giggles like a young girl. "Don't tell your mother I told you," she repeats. "She doesn't like to give away family secrets."

We cross the creek again, and head up the path to Reba's house. Another family story, another family secret. I think about what my aunt told me, and how it connected to another story my mom had whispered to me more than thirty years ago. I was in high school, coming home late from a weekend party; mom was up, sitting at the kitchen table, brushes in hand, working on an oil painting.

She was a wonderful artist, but with kids and a house to manage, she rarely had time to paint. Sometimes, she'd get the urge and she'd stay up all night, when the house was quiet and she knew she wouldn't be interrupted. She'd drink pot after pot of coffee, unaware of the time until the morning light came through the window.

That night, she was in a talkative mood and whispered stories over her coffee cup. "I never knew for sure if Aunt Joy and Aunt Jean Ann belonged to my father. Mom would just get tired of us and disappear for a while. By the time I was in high school, I just hated her, and when she left I hoped she'd never come back. But Daddy always let her come home. I never knew why."

She picked up her brush again, fairly stabbing the paint onto her canvas, her eyes veiled once again. I went up to bed, feeling her sadness, sensing I'd just been allowed to see a glimmer of the raw hurt she always kept locked away. In the morning, a delicate landscape sat on the little easel on the kitchen table, and Mom never mentioned that story again.

As my grandmother got older and more fragile, Mom showed an immense and tender love toward her that betrayed no trace of disappointment or hurt. Grandma's last months had been hard; her youngest son, my Uncle Chuck, died of cancer just months before her own death. He was the second child my grandmother had buried that year; my Aunt Joy had died just weeks before.

My grandmother had eight children, and she had seen four of them die. After my uncle's funeral, mom told me she knew her mother would soon be gone. "When I saw her sitting in her wheelchair, all hunched over, staring at her hands during the service, I knew she was ready." As always, Mom had been right.

The night of my grandmother's funeral, my parents and I have dinner, just us, away from all the cousins and aunts and friends in town. Mom tells us about staying behind at the gravesite with her sisters after everyone else had left. "We just sat there and talked to Mom," she says.

"She'd had such a hard time after Joy and Chuckie died, and I knew she was happy where she was. She was finally at peace. I'm going to miss her, but I don't feel sad anymore."

I tell her about finding Uncle Luther's newspapers in the shack that morning, and she giggles. "He was so secretive. He never liked anyone knowing his business," she remembers. "He kept all his stories locked in a chest. One night my brother Bo and I broke into it and read a story called *White Shoulders*. When he found out, he beat us with a switch out on the porch." She smiles, the corners of her big brown eyes crinkling at the memory. "My mother just said, 'Serves you right.'"

The next morning, I knock on the door between our adjoining hotel rooms to say good-bye before driving back to the airport. Mom hugs me hard, speaking quick and quiet again. "I'm glad you were here. You made it so much easier for me. I love you."

Her vulnerability nearly makes me cry. During the eulogy, I'd joked that my grandmother would just as soon smack you upside the head than give you a kiss. Everyone laughed; they knew Miss Hattie. She could be fierce, but she had a deeply sentimental side, and as she got older, she made no bones about grabbing her children and grandchildren to love 'em up. The last time I'd seen her, we'd sat in rockers, side by side, and she'd gripped my hand like she'd never let go, smiling with joy just because one of her grandsons was around.

Grandma's outer toughness and inner vulnerability were traits she passed on to my mother. When we were kids, Mom scared the daylights out of my siblings and me. She was tough and strict and could make us quake just by looking at us. But we knew, somehow, there was a tender heart underneath. We'd catch a glimpse of it when she was around dogs and little babies. But it wasn't until she had grandchildren that she really began wearing her heart on her sleeve.

She loved and spoiled all my nieces like nobody's business; and when Michael and I decided to adopt, all she said was, "Give me some grandsons."

She fell in love with the boys the first time she met them, and they with her. Maybe it was because she was the first grandmother they'd ever known, or maybe it was because they had a sense that she, like them, had a mother who abandoned her. Whatever the reason, the bond was quick and strong.

Last summer, they stayed with her and my father for a week during summer vacation. When I picked them up to fly back home, they told Grandma stories for hours, concluding, "You're just like Grandma. She gets mad and swears a lot, too!" When they teased her about it, she laughed, giving them permission to call her a special nickname they all kept secret. Today I finally pry it out of her.

Just as I am about to drive away to the airport, she opens the door of her hotel room. Giggling, she calls out, "Tell the boys their Grandma Shit loves them!"

# Little Michael's Online Adventures

When Dereck asks me to help him format his book report, I sit down at Little Michael's computer to review what he has written. "This is good, honey!" The sentences are clean, and he's already gone through and fixed spelling errors. "I don't see anything I'd change."

"How do you make it double spaced?" he asks.

"Here's how you format it that way." In a flash, it is done. That's when I notice the button on the bottom of the screen, one of the Internet links that had been saved when Little Michael was Net surfing. One click confirms the worst.

It is a graphic pornography site.

"Dereck, do me a favor. Go ask Daddy Michael to come down here, and close the door on your way out." Seeing my face, he doesn't ask any questions. He runs out to get Michael. As soon as the door closes, I double-click. In seconds, two bizarre creatures are on the screen, engaged in activity that even I find a bit scary.

Quickly, I click off and look at the history of sites visited. Little Michael had figured out how to modify the history, so it only shows sites visited over the last two days. But it is enough. Interspersed with at least a dozen porn sites are visits to a Yahoo e-mail address that isn't familiar to me.

Daddy Michael comes in and closes the door behind him.

"He's into chicks with dicks," I tell him.

"Oh, crap." He sits down on the edge of the bed. "Are you sure?"

"Either that or one of the dogs is sneaking in at night to learn a new trick or two. And he's got an e-mail account when we told him he wasn't allowed."

"I knew we should have renewed NetNanny."

"Well, we didn't think we needed to. Dumb us. We'd better talk to him."

Even before he walks into his room and closes the door, Little Michael knows he is in trouble. "What did I do?"

"Michael, have you been looking at pornography on the Internet?"

He turns white. "No. No."

"Would someone else have been in your room on Tuesday night, after you were supposed to be in bed?"

"No."

"Then how do you explain the fact that someone looked at a dozen porn sites on this computer on Tuesday night alone? Was it you?"

He twists and bites his lip and stares at his fingers. "No …" Then he starts to cry. "I'm so embarrassed."

"Was it you? Yes or no?" I'm not about to let up on him.

"Yes." His voice trails off.

"Do you have an e-mail account?"

"No."

"Then who is mikey2brady? Whoever that person is was going back and forth between porn and their mailbox all night. Is it you?"

"I don't have an e-mail account. I told you."

"I don't believe you. What's the password?"

"I don't have a password."

"What's the password, Michael?"

He chews on his lips some more, before muttering something under his breath.

"What did you say? I didn't hear you."

"Patriots."

"That's your password?"

He nods, and I log into the account. There are 1,320 unread messages. Most are addressed to "wemenlover" from an adult online dating service.

"Who's wemenlover?"

"I don't know."

"If you don't, why have you gotten over a thousand e-mails to that person on your Yahoo account?"

"I don't read them."

"They didn't appear out of nowhere. When did you sign up for this?"

"I don't know." With that he collapses on his bed and covers his face with hands.

He lays on his bed as we look at him and at each other. What do we say and what do we do?

We let him cry for a few moments; it gives us time to think. Finally, I look at him. "Michael, I need you to sit up now and pay attention."

Blubbering, he slowly sits up, but he won't look at us. His long hair covers his eyes and face, a protective shield. *Jesus, it's way past time for him to get a haircut,* I think.

"Okay, Michael. Here's the deal. I'm disappointed you're looking at porn, but you're at the age where you're curious, and I can understand why you'd want to see it. What I have a big problem with is that you've lied to us again. We asked you this summer if you'd been looking, and you lied so convincingly we believed you. And today, you tried to lie about it again, and you tried to lie about having an e-mail account. That's the much bigger problem for us."

I pause to let it sink in. "Do you remember what Daddy Michael told you last summer about why you shouldn't look at porn online?"

He nods.

"What did he say?"

Little Michael mumbles, but at least we can hear him. "He said porn sites had viruses that could mess up your computer. And that people who e-mailed from porn sites might be dangerous. They could be adults pretending to be kids, and they might want to hurt kids."

Daddy Michael looks down at him. "I'm really impressed you remembered that, Michael. But I'm not impressed you didn't listen to me and that you've lied again."

I continue. "Michael, I'm also disappointed you feel like you can't tell us the truth about things you are interested in and want to know. Sex and love are incredibly important things, and going to the Internet may not get you information that can help you. In fact, it can lead you to things that might not help you at all."

He continues to snuffle on his bed, still wrapped in a ball.

"I want to make sure you understand something. It's normal and natural and perfectly okay to want to know about sex and love. In fact, it would be weird if you weren't thinking about it. I can see why you might be embarrassed and not want to talk about this. But it's important to get good information, and sometimes you've got to get over being embarrassed to get the things you need."

He looks up at us, his face still wet.

"So why don't you do this. Take some time to think about the questions you have, and bring them up to us so we can talk about them. We're not experts, but we can share what we know, or at least help you get answers if we don't know. Ask whatever you want. The best way to learn is to ask about what you want to know."

He shakes his head. "I'm too embarrassed."

"It's okay to be embarrassed, but that's not the point. You want to know stuff, right?"

He nods.

"Then focus on what you want to know and not on feeling embarrassed. Bring us five questions later today. And we'll think about what the consequences will be for your lying to us. Agreed?"

Reluctantly, he nods again. We leave the room and close his door.

Half an hour later, he trudges up to the office and lays down a sheet of paper in front of me. I keep my face impassive as I read. But inside I'm thinking, *Oh, thank God. At least I think I can answer these!*

"Do you want to talk about your questions, honey?"

His eyes roll ever so slightly, but he nods and sits down.

He continues to roll his eyes periodically over the next few minutes as we speak—just a teenager's natural reflex in the face of embarrassing information. It's not the easiest conversation we've ever had, but it's not too awkward or painful, either. And he sits without fidgeting, which is remarkable.

When he leaves the room, Daddy Michael and I look at each other and sigh, suddenly very, very tired. "What do you think?" I ask.

"I wish my parents had done that with me," he says.

"Me, too."

We're going to have to come up with a darned good consequence for lying to us, but if he learns anything from us, I want him to know there is no topic or question that is ever off limits for discussion. Hopefully, the fascination with chicks and dicks is just a passing phase, like checking out the store windows at Macy's before deciding what to buy for Christmas.

I'm still not sure we're handling this the right way. We can only do the best we can. But if we can help Michael learn how to better deal with all the confusion his natural curiosity will bring him, if we can help Michael feel comfortable talking about what's on his mind, that will put him far, far ahead of where either of us were at his age.

And if he's really, really lucky, maybe this will save him a lot of money in therapist bills some time down the road.

## Is My Mother Dead?

We're grabbing a hurried lunch at the Hippopotamus restaurant across from the Gare de Nord train station in Paris, hoping we can get served before we catch the Eurostar back to London. It's Thanksgiving Day, near the end of our first European trip as a family, and the boys are wound up.

They're wiggling and jumping in their chairs, full of energy after a long car ride into Paris from the Loire Valley, where we'd visited cousins who run a cooking school in their four-hundred-year old chateau. The boys had spent the day before playing football in the pea-graveled gardens and running down corridors looking for ghosts among the chateau's thirty-two bedrooms. We'd spent an extra hour crammed into the small car trying to find the entrance to the car rental return near the train station this morning, and they are so wound up they are about to burst.

Suddenly, Little Michael turns to me and asks, "Is my mother dead?

Little Michael's question is the last thing I expect from a boy whose sole focus seemed to be learning to play tiddly-winks with the big English tuppence coins he found in his pocket. But he looks up at me expectantly, confident I can answer his question.

"I don't know. Why do you ask?"

"I don't know. The last time we saw her, she didn't look too good, and she was using drugs and stuff."

"How would you feel about that, Michael? Would you be upset?"

He shrugs. "I dunno." He takes his straw and flicks some water at his youngest brother, and in an instant, his attention completely turns to flipping the copper coins again.

The suddenness of this exchange takes my breath away. Stunned, I look across the table to Daddy Michael. I mouth, "Did you hear what he asked me?" He shakes his head no, just as the waitress delivers our food. "French fries!" the boys cry, grabbing them by the handfuls as soon as they're placed on the table.

Once we're on the train and the boys are absorbed in their Gameboys and PSPs, I recount the conversation to Daddy Michael. "What do you think triggered that question? He's not brought her up for months."

"Who knows? But I'm glad we know he's thinking about it. I certainly have."

Even though Little Michael doesn't raise the issue again, I know he's not completely worked this through. We mention his comment to a therapist friend after we get back. She suggests his question is a metaphor for the death of his mother as a parental figure; he's unconsciously making the transition, acknowledging us as the parents who are there to take care of him.

That could be—slowly over the past few months, he has begun to let those feelings out. He is a gentle soul, but more than once, he's said in a very quiet voice, "I'm mad at my mother for not trying to keep us." That's as far as he can bring himself before he closes up again. There's no yelling, no tears, no heat around the words, just a solemn acknowledgement of feelings he has long suppressed.

A couple of weeks later, we're having lunch with our friend Amy, a children's rights attorney. "How would we found out if their mom died?"

"The only way is to check thorough a website like Vital Records and ask for a death certificate," she said. "I wish there was a simpler way, but there's not. You wouldn't believe all the steps we have to go through to try to find parents who have disappeared from their kids' lives."

Daddy Michael and I talk about whether or not we should check, but intuitively, we both sense that she is still around. I don't know what it is, but it's something like being able to sense a storm brewing on the horizon. You just know.

And the boys, somehow, sense it, too. While Michael knows but can't talk about how he feels, Dereck can express himself without completely understanding what's he's feeling. He's the yin to Michael's yang. We've learned that one triggers the other.

The week of Dereck's birthday in mid-December, the social worker calls to tell us that their mom has called her to ask about the boys; what can she tell her about their lives now? I share a few stories and give her an update, and tell her to remind mom she can write to them at the post office box we've set up.

And I wait, knowing that even if we don't tell the boys that she's made contact, they'll somehow sense it. Dereck is the bellwether. He's got an innate psychic connection to her. Every time she's made contact, we see a big shift in his behavior.

Sure as rain, Dereck falls into the doldrums. It doesn't help that one of the boys who came to his birthday sleepover got sick that night, and Dereck and three of the other boys quickly came down with the same virus. With a 103-degree fever, Dereck withdraws into himself, spending his birthday in bed, a deep frown on his face.

No amount of hugging or cuddling or cajoling can get him out of his depression. And he gets mean: he snaps at his brothers, fights with his friends, and acts sullen and unresponsive with us. He has a play date with his best friend Giacomo, and when we pick him up, he opens the door and pushes past us without a greeting.

Of course, his behavior drives me crazy. There's nothing I can't stand more than a sullen kid. "Dereck, what's wrong?"

"Nu-ting." Dereck's got a slight speech impediment, and has a hard time with the letter "h," especially when he's pulled down the corners of his mouth into a frown.

This goes on for days; we alternate between cuddling him and scolding him, trying to get him to open up and share his obvious misery. Finally, when the three boys are playing Xbox, he gets mad and punches Matthew. High drama ensues.

Matthew cries and runs to me. I can tell in an instant he's not really hurt, but Dereck's just broken cardinal rule number one: don't hit your brothers. I swoop in.

"Turn off the game right now. What's going on?"

"Matthew's laughing at me because he beat me at Halo."

"And you think that is an excuse to hit your brother?"

"He wouldn't leave me alone. He kept bothering me." Dereck curls up into the couch, his cheeks red. I can feel Matthew gloating behind me.

"You know that hitting your brother is completely unacceptable. I'm surprised at you, Dereck. You should know better. Go to your room and get ready for bed right now."

Dereck slams down his control and stomps off to bed. As he walks by Matthew, I hear Matthew whisper "Hee-hee" almost under his breath, a wicked, triumphant grin on his face.

"Matthew, that's it. You too. Get ready for bed."

I give them a couple of minutes, and then go into their room. Dereck is sobbing on his bed while Matthew stands near the closet door half in his pajamas, frightened.

"Dereck, what's wrong?" I try to keep my voice neutral, but I've had enough of his shenanigans over the past week.

"I … just … miss … my mom." He turns his head into his pillow, wailing.

I think, *Thank God, we've finally had a breakthrough.* I sit down on the bed next to him, and he immediately wraps his arm around me and puts his head in my lap. He's finally reaching out.

There's no privacy in our house. Matthew lies in his bunk, listening attentively with his head hanging over the side, just above my head. Little Michael, standing outside the door eavesdropping, ventures in and sits on the floor near the bed. They know this conversation is going to be good, and they're not about to miss it.

"Honey, I'm sorry you miss your mom. I know how much that hurts." He snuggles in closer. "Is that what's been bothering you for the last week?" He nods.

"You've made yourself very unhappy all week, and you've been mean to everyone around you. Were you trying to make everyone else as unhappy as you were?"

He looks up at me, just a bit quizzical, and shakes his head no.

"Remember the conversations we've had about your mom? Do you remember how much she loves you but can't take care of you because of her disease?" He nods again. "It is really sad that she can't take care of you. I know how much you miss her. But if you just focus on that, you're always going to be unhappy. Are there things that make you happy?"

He thinks for a minute, and the nods again.

"Like what?"

"Our family. Our dogs. My friends at school. Playing football."

"Well, whenever you get stuck feeling bad, it always helps to think about the things that make you happy. It's really sad that your mom couldn't take care of you and you aren't able to live with her. But God was really watching out for you."

Dereck is listening intently.

I continue, "Do you know what the word blessing means?" He shakes his head no. "I think God was blessing you. He knew you would need extra special help since you didn't have your mom, and he took good care of you by giving you the things you needed: parents who love you, a nice home to live in, a chance to be with your brothers, your dogs, and in a great school."

He nods, and I can see he is thinking hard about what I'm saying. "So when you're feeling really bad, you have a choice. You can focus on the thing that makes you feel bad and be miserable, or you can focus on the good things God's given you. If you do that, I bet you would feel a lot better."

"When I play with Mo, I feel better."

"That's a great start. You always have to remind yourself of the fact that you have two dads and two brothers and four dogs who really, really love you."

"I know." He snuggles for a moment longer, then moves to curl up around his pillow.

"Do you want to sleep?"

He nods again.

I ask, "Do you want to say a prayer for your mom before you go to sleep?"

He nods again, and all the boys move in. We join hands as I look at Matthew, and he instinctively starts, "Thank you, God, for our family and for our dogs and please take care of our mom."

Little Michael adds a resounding, "Yeah!" and all the boys giggle.

"I think that covers it," I laugh, and we all say "Amen."

I kiss Dereck good night, tuck Matthew into the bunk above him, and turn out the light. Dereck sleeps for fourteen hours and wakes up sunny and smiling. The storm has passed.

## It's A Guy Thing, Part I

Moments after ripping open their Christmas packages, our three boys have left the piles of wrapping paper and gifts and moved to the garage, where they assemble the two toy airplanes their Uncle Malcolm sent them from New Jersey.

"There's a CD and a manual that tells you how to fly them," I begin.

"We know what to do!" They mutter among themselves, arguing about which piece goes where and how many rubber bands are attached to each wing. "No! It goes there! Put it there."

We've barely had the time to fill garbage bags with torn wrapping paper before they rush back in, clamoring to go to Balboa Park, where there's a special field to fly planes. "Did you look at the CD with the instructions?" I ask again.

"We know what to do!" They exude all the confidence of youth, and soon, we're piling into the minivan. Michael and I have already bet a Starbucks latte over how long it will take before they crash both planes. I give them five minutes; he says it will be less than two.

I give it one last try as we're driving. "You know, it might be a good idea to look at the directions in the manual before we get there."

"Daddy John, we know what to do."

The park is filled with experienced flyers. They're all middle-aged men with huge toolboxes, tinkering with their planes on the picnic tables at the edge of the field. The whir of their planes and their laughing banter fill the air. Eager when they piled out the car, the boys are suddenly intimidated—they don't want to mess up in front of a bunch of men who know what they are doing.

But the men are great. They welcome our sons and clear a space for them to lay out their planes on one of the tables. Soon, they're all calling out often-contrary instructions.

"It's too windy today for the size of your planes!"

"It's a perfect day. Just fly directly into the wind!"

"Set the control this way."

"No, don't listen to that old fart. Do it this way!"

Michael and I stand on the edge of the group, watching. "Notice not one of them tells them to read the directions," I mutter to Michael. "It's definitely a guy thing. We just don't like to be told what to do."

Little Michael goes first. With his brothers and their new comrades shouting and laughing behind, he plays with the controls, trying to get the plane into the air. It slowly lifts off the field, rising about twenty feet before it does a quick tailspin and plummets back down. The wing cracks on impact.

His crestfallen face says it all. "Does anyone have any tape?" he asks as he runs his plane back to the table.

Dereck doesn't fare much better. He manages to get the plane up briefly before it does a somersault and dives nose first into the ground. Surveying the damage, he asks, "Anyone got some rubber bands?"

"Looks like you won the latte," I say to Michael. The boys and their new friends cluster around the planes, tinkering and arguing about the best ways to fix them. I glance down at the manual in my hand and slowly put it my jacket pocket. They won't need it.

Watching them, I think about how angry I got trying to change the clock in the car after daylight savings time. I'd sat in the driveway for an hour cursing and fuming before I figured out the answer. It never occurred to me to look at the manual in the glove compartment. I had to figure out it for myself. Why should our boys be any different?

Yep, it's definitely a guy thing.

## It's A Guy Thing, Part II

"Can we take our planes to Richard's house? He wants to see them!"

"You can't fly them in his neighborhood. There are too many cars and people and houses. Got it?"

"Okay, okay."

It's Christmas afternoon. After their run at Balboa Park, we stop at home to feed the dogs and change clothes. We're heading to our friend Tracy's house for a Christmas party at her neighbors. Tracy's son Richard is twelve, and he hangs out all the time with Little Michael and Dereck. We call him our number-four son, which he loves. Since our boys got their planes, he's started working on his mom to get one for him.

Tracy had called as we were driving home from the park. "I just wanted to give you a head's up, doll. I'm getting slightly dressed up for this party. I know you'd want to know." That's her gracious code for telling me to make sure the boys are in clean clothes and that Daddy Michael's shaved; her neighbor sets great store on propriety.

This is the first time this season we've been invited to anything requiring us to dress, and it feels good to pull out nice clothes. There's something about the holidays that calls for dressing up. Little Michael and Dereck help me pick out the right cuff links to go with my shirt and jacket.

Rummaging through the pile in my new cuff link box, their Christmas gift to me, they decide on Russian blue enamel rectangles, edged in silver, with silver profiles of the last tsar and tsarina. Dereck has an eye for detail and is very confident about the choice.

"Look, Daddy John. The blue matches that blue stripe in your shirt."

The backings are a bit tight, so little Michael helps me get them on. He looks up and smiles. "These are cool, Daddy John." They hate to dress up themselves, but they like their dad to look good.

Tracy's street is a blaze of competitive Christmas lighting. People from all over the city drive up and down her neighborhood during the holidays, pointing out the millions of lights festooning the houses, trees, shrubs, and holiday lawn ornaments on nearly every property. It's so bright that the valet at Tracy's neighbor's house doesn't even have to turn on cars' headlights to park along the street.

We have cocktails in Tracy's living room before heading over. Joan, Tracy's mom, is visiting from New Jersey, and Charley, the man she's been dating for a few months, is there, too. We love Joan and like Charley a lot. "He's a keeper," I told Tracy the first time we met him.

Little Michael asks for the van keys to get the plane out to show Richard. We hand over the keys, and I give him a look. "I know, I know," he mutters before running out the front door.

We five adults laugh together, enjoying a brief respite from the kids. But it's not long before Richard comes in and asks his mother to join him the kitchen. He looks down, not daring to glance in our direction. It's all I need. I casually follow them.

Richard's face is frightened when he sees me. "It's my fault. I did it. I flew the plane into the tree."

"Didn't the boys tell you we told them not to fly it in the neighborhood?"

He nods. "I'm sorry. It's my fault. I wanted to fly it."

"No, Richard, it's not. They knew better, and they shouldn't have let you."

Tracy watches our interaction, bemused. "Well, we can just get a ladder and pull it down."

"Where is it, Richard?" I ask.

"It's in a tree down the street. It's pretty high up. You almost can't see it."

"Let's go have a look."

Charley has come into the kitchen behind me and says, "I'll go with you."

When we open the front door, our three boys are on the porch, waiting. I just look at them as I walk past; they know they are in trouble. "Where's the plane?"

We walk down the street to a home five doors down, to one of the few houses on the street that isn't lit up like a Christmas tree. Richard points. "It's up there. In the branches, almost over the street."

The lights from the houses nearby are just enough to illuminate the plane, high in a branch near the top of the tree.

Richard asks, "Should I go get the ladder?"

I shake my head no and take off my shoes. Quickly, I pull myself up into the tree, and climb, branch after branch, until I can reach the plane's wing. "Michael, catch the plane when I drop it," I say. He lifts his arms and catches it. They all wait until I drop down, wipe off my pants, and put on my shoes.

Richard's mouth is agape. "Whoa," he says. "You just shot up that tree like Spiderman."

"Never underestimate a pissed off dad," I tell him as we walk back to the house.

"So, boys, what should be the consequence for this little stunt?" I ask. I'm grouchy and short-tempered with them, but underneath, I'm biting the inside of my cheeks. Of course they were going to fly the plane again. And of course, they'd fly it into something. I'm just glad it wasn't into the windshield of an oncoming car.

They all hang their heads, embarrassed. "Uh, are you going to take the planes away?"

"Daddy Michael and I are going to have to discuss this. I'm pretty disappointed you didn't listen to us. And glad you didn't cause any serious damage. Why do you think we told you not to fly the plane in a neighborhood?"

They don't say anything, but they can feel me staring them down. Finally, Little Michael says, "Uh, so we don't hit something and stuff?"

"You're right. So why did you?"

"We just wanted to."

"And you didn't care about the potential consequences."

"Yeah." If their heads were any lower, they'd be dragging their noses on the ground. There's a fine line between influencing their behavior through guilt and encouraging them to think before they do something that is potentially dangerous. I'm walking that line, and I have to admit that the tired, worn-out parent side of me just wants them to feel guilty.

I know I'll regret it later, but I can't stop myself. "Hey, Michael," I continue. "What was it that your mom used to say to you?"

He mumbles into his shirt, "Think before you do."

"She was a smart woman," I respond. "Daddy Michael and I will talk to you about the consequences tomorrow. Until then, I want you to think about what they should be."

As we get to Tracy's front door, Charley whispers in my ear, "Nice. They're going to worry about it all night."

I grin at him. "That's the whole point."
We both laugh and go in to finish our drinks.

## New Year's Resolution

My Grinch-o-meter is definitely tilting in the wrong direction. Nearly three weeks in to their Christmas holiday, I am counting every second until the boys go back to school.

I'm tired of little heads peering over my shoulder as I work, trying to read my computer screen because they're bored.

I'm tired of napping through wretched movies like *Cheaper by the Dozen Two* and *Fun with Dick and Jane* to keep the kids occupied for a few hours.

I'm tired of making cheesy eggs and peanut butter sandwiches and picking up half-empty soda cans around the house.

I'm tired of ornaments falling off the dried-out Christmas tree and rolling across the floor to become chew toys for our Bernese puppy.

And I'm most tired of hearing "I'm bored," the constant, singsong mantra that gets louder and more insistent with each passing day.

But even as I grumble, I realize it is not the boys' fault that I'm so cranky. It's not the chronic boredom, the bickering, or the messes that make the entire house look like Little Michael's bedroom. It's the mess of our own making that is getting to me.

A year ago, the boys were still adjusting to their new home, and it was easy to attribute any bad behaviors to their birth parents. Now, when we see something we don't like, we have no one to blame but ourselves.

All through this holiday, I can't escape the nagging feeling that we are spoiling our boys rotten. They've lost the capacity to amuse themselves; they sulk and pout and get irritable if we're not ready to go the hobby store, buy them a Starbucks chocolate chip Frappachino, or run them to the arcade to spend a small fortune on video games whenever the whim strikes.

I wonder when we crossed the line between being good providers and overindulging. We've become the kind of parents I used to deride back before we knew better.

Mind you, we had good motives—we knew how difficult their lives had been before meeting us, and we wanted to make up for that. We wanted to give them the experiences and opportunities to see there was a whole world beyond the trailer park and home meth lab, to see themselves as universal citizens who could expect good from what had always been a harsh world.

But somewhere along the way, we managed to go too far, and now there's an overcorrection to be made. I'm tempted to run downstairs, turn off the TV and video games, and yell, "Get outside and play! I don't want to see your faces until dark!"

But that voice wouldn't be me. It was what my mom used to say to my siblings and me when we were insufferable, and my boys would see through it in a minute. Little Michael, who likes to eavesdrop when I call to complain to my mother, would just cock his head and ask, "Have you been talking to Grandma again?"

Our boys' spoiled behavior has nothing to do with them and everything to do with us.

So, just how do you break the habit of doing everything for your kids so they can learn to do on their own?

I get a clue when I'm hired to do a media training for a family participating on a new reality series on TLC. The three children lived on sugar, and the parents never connected their screaming and tantrums and bad behavior to nutrition. An "expert" had come into their household and announced the kids were consuming 132 times the amount of sugar they needed each day. The horrified parents happily accepted a series of rules that included eliminating sugar. After a few days of tears and whining, the kids, too, settled down and actually embraced the new rules. And their behavior problems disappeared.

The mom had never done interviews before, so we started with a mock-interview to assess how well she'd answer questions. I asked her if following the rules had been hard. She thought for a moment, and grinned. "No. The rules were powerful. They gave us the structure we needed, and it gave us as parents the power back we'd lost."

The light bulb went off in my head, and after we finished, I took her aside and thanked her, "You've just helped me figure out a big dilemma with my own kids."

She smiled an enormous smile. "I'm so glad! That gives me more confidence than anything we've done all day!"

It was all about structure, the very thing we knew was so important to the boys after the inconsistency of their prior life. We had given them a lot of basics, like doing homework immediately after school, making their beds in the morning, and setting limits on TV and video games.

That worked during school, but we slacked off during vacations. We thought they needed a break. We let things degenerate into an easy free-for-all. No firm bedtimes, no clear limits on TV, no requirements to read or study or improve their brains. It made perfect sense they would push to figure out their boundaries. Suddenly, what had seemed like an insurmountable challenge looked fixable.

We had an immediate opportunity to provide a little more structure that night. Little Michael obsesses about things he wants and is relentless in their pursuit. He'd worked on us to give him a drum set, two guitars, a hamster, and an endless stream of toys. Lately, he's been obsessing about having an iguana, and it came up again at the dinner table.

"Michael, what's involved in taking care of an iguana?"

"I dunno. You got to feed it and stuff."

"Well, if you want an iguana, that's something you should look at. You're taking on the responsibility to care for another living creature, and you've got to be prepared."

"I know I can take care of it."

"Honey, they need a very specific kind of environment and a specific diet and they also need exercise. You need to know what's required. And you also need to look at your willingness to make that commitment."

"I'll do it."

"The best way to look at if you can handle more responsibility is to look at how you handle responsibility now. We constantly remind you to feed your hamster and clean the cage. If you want another animal, you've got to show us you can handle the responsibility by taking better care of your hamster and being consistent with the other things you're supposed to do."

He grimaces. "But I clean the cage."

I look at him. "Michael, when was the last time you cleaned your hamster's cage?"

He shrugs. "I dunno."

"It was before Thanksgiving, when I asked you to clean it before Aunt Tracy came to dinner. That was more than six weeks ago. The cage smells, and your room stinks. That doesn't show me you're being responsible."

"But what if I clean the cage?"

"It's a good start. Why don't we make a list of the responsibilities you have, and you can use it as a checklist. If you can show us you are being responsible for at least a month, we can have the conversation about buying an iguana again."

"Awww. Okay."

After dinner, we sit down and make out the list, covering everything from doing homework to practicing his guitar to taking out the trashcans each Thursday. At first, he seems agitated, not wanting to deal with it. But as we make the list and talk about the time involved and what needs to be done when, he begins to relax. He realizes this is something he can do, and the structure is something he can live with.

The funny thing is, the process makes us both feel better. The Grinch-o-meter in my head just disappears, replaced by a sense that I'm doing something positive to help my son. Little Michael starts the new year off with a renewed sense of purpose, more aware and quick to say, "Daddy John, did you see that I picked up the clothes on my floor this morning? See, I'm being more responsible."

"Yes, I did, honey, and I really appreciate it. And don't you feel good about it, too?"

He blushes a bit, shrugs his shoulders, and says, "Yeah, I guess so." But underneath the shrug, I can see he's even more pleased with himself than I am. Lesson learned: a little bit of structure goes a long way.

# Teaching Morality

Every morning, the boys and I wind our way through a deluge of traffic on Highland Avenue to the Hollywood Schoolhouse. On Mondays, the boys bicker and tease each other, kicking the seats with pent up energy. As the week progresses, the noise and activity begins to fade. By Friday, they sit silent, staring out the window, faces cloudy with leftover sleep, waiting to recharge their batteries again over the weekend.

In the car, I listen to NPR. One of the first mornings we drove together, Dereck asked me, "Daddy John, why do you always listen to the news?"

"I like to know what's going on in the world," I told him. If the story connects to something they're interested in, they listen, too. When Hurricane Katrina struck, they were glued to the radio, filled with questions about whether Los Angeles could flood and what we could do to help all the stranded dogs.

Matthew, the youngest, tends to pay the least attention. Grown-up stories are not for him. But he's already formed a lot of opinions, especially about politics. If he hears an audio clip of the president, he screams from the back seat, "Boo, Bush!"

We're not shy about expressing our political views around the kids, but the first time Matthew erupted in the car like that, my head did a near 180-degree turn. "Honey, why did you say that?"

"Because he started a war and hurt people and didn't have to," he said.

"Where did you learn that?"

"Deshon and Rodrigo talked about it in school. They said Bush is a bad man."

"Is that what you think, too?"

"Yes." He voice was firm and emphatic. "You don't like Bush either, Daddy John." It was more of a statement than a question.

"No, honey, I don't."

"Good." My opinion seemed to validate his, and before he got out of the car to walk into school, he reached up, rubbed my bald head, and giggled. He does that sometimes at dinner, or when I'm tucking him into bed or after we've had a conversation he thinks important. The first time he did it, I wondered, *Does my head look like Buddha's belly?* But now I know it's a sign of connection more than good luck.

When you inherit kids, they come with a lot of things preordained. Attitudes and interests and reactions are already firmly established, as are their moral values. Even at five, Matthew had a clear sense of what he believed was right and wrong. As new parents, we had the double challenge of figuring out what he and his brothers already believed while trying to impart the values we hope they would adopt as their own.

The polarization in this country has made that challenge even more complicated. When I was in school, we had lively classroom discussions about morality and how belief systems were formed. But that doesn't seem to happen anymore; things have changed. Morality is often a code word for extremism, and words like faith and values and hope, once burnished and cherished as common to all people, are simply triggers for enmity and dissent.

The fact that we're a family headed by two dads who happen to love each other is enough to make some people call us moral degenerates and want to tear our kids away from us. Sometimes it's hard not to take the rhetoric personally; I want to tell the folks who think moral absolutes were written on clay tablets to go jump in the lake. But that feels like responding to hate with hate. Somehow, that would diminish the powerful love that has grown within our family.

Still, it means we don't have access to some of the traditional avenues parents pursue to build strong values in their children; kids need a moral compass to help them with the decisions they make every day. How do we teach our sons to decide what is right or wrong? How do they decide whether or not to cheat on a spelling test, take the last cookie on the plate, or taunt a classmate they don't like?

Our boys need guidelines they can live with. Daddy Michael and I talk about taking the boys to a nondenominational church or synagogue so they have some experience with a community of people who share common values and beliefs. Daddy Michael grew up a cultural Jew and has never been involved in an organized faith, but now he's ready to give it a try, convinced it would be good for the boys.

The funny thing is, I'm not. I grew up Catholic, embraced Evangelical Protestantism when I was in college, and was asked to leave my church when I figured out I was gay and was not willing to live a life of abstinence. It was heart-wrenching when it happened, and I still can't hear certain hymns without tearing up. I miss the comfort and the community and the sense of belonging.

I'm terribly gun-shy. I don't ever want them in a situation where they might someday have to turn away from something they love because it is fundamentally incompatible with who they are.

And I don't want to make them contend with absolutes that don't make sense. They've already had to sort out too many things in their lives that were painful and confusing. What they've gone through has made them gentle souls, sensitive to the pain of others, and their compassion knows no bounds.

Dereck can't pass a homeless person without wanting to give him money. Michael takes great care to describe people kindly and corrects friends when they don't. When some boys in the schoolyard were picking on Matthew's classmates, Julianna and Lena, he jumped right in to stop them and got punched in the face for his effort. Julianna's mom called us to tell us Matthew was a hero that day.

Without knowing it, they live by the Golden Rule. And I am deathly afraid that exposure to organized religion will wipe away the instinctive goodness each already carries.

So we'll have to do the best we can without the support of a church or congregation. We pray with Matthew every night. He sometimes puts his little hand on the stubble covering my bald head, and his prayers are pure and honest and directed to a God he knows is watching over him. We put the boys in a great school that embraces the values we believe are important; we surround them with friends and family who approach the world with love and service. We try to create our own community to nurture and cultivate and set an example for our boys.

And we hope. I know history goes in cycles, and I know this dark cycle will pass. Maybe, someday—not in our lifetimes perhaps, but in the lifetimes of our sons—we'll live again in a place where faith and morals and goodness are no longer tainted by the brush of extremism, where each of us can be embraced fully for all that we are.

## Nasty Girls

"Those nasty girls got in trouble last night in Larchmont," Little Michael blurts out as he climbs into the car. He leans over and hugs me once he's in his seat. I back out of our friend Tracy's driveway onto the tree-lined, quiet street in the idyllic neighborhood where Tracy lives with her son Richard and daughter Taylor. Michael's spent the night with Tracy's son Richard and their friend River.

"What happened?"

Michael, Richard, River, and another friend, Jonathan, formed a garage band, and Tracy offered her family room as a place to practice. There's a gang of neighborhood girls—groupies, really—that congregates in the family room whenever the boys practice, and from everything Michael says, they're nothing but trouble. It doesn't help that Shannon, one of the girls, has a crush on Michael, and like any teenage girl who can't get the attention of a shy boy, she taunts him like nobody's business.

"They were sniffing Dust-Off and stuff, and when they went to Larchmont, they got caught."

I don't get it. "They were sniffing what?"

"Dust-Off. The stuff you use for your computer."

"They were sniffing that? Where?"

"At Tracy's house. I didn't see it, though. But it's supposed to get you high. And they were sniffing lighter fluid, too. Then they got sick on the sidewalk in Larchmont."

"If you didn't see it, how do you know they were doing it?"

"That's what they told their parents, and the parents called Aunt Tracy. Boy, was she mad. The girls can't come over anymore." He smiles, pleased at the outcome. "Those girls are nasty."

When we get home, I call Tracy. She'd been making dinner and had no idea the girls were ransacking her office, where they found the Dust-off and started inhaling it. "When they headed upstairs to use the bathroom in a pack, I should have known better," she tells me. "It never occurred to me I'd need to lock up office products. But I guess that doesn't matter now. That was the last time those girls come into my house."

As I hang up, I see Little Michael has been listening. "They're just nasty. They do stupid stuff all the time. I don't know why Richard likes to hang out with them."

"Why do you think Richard invites them over?"

"He just likes them. He's always talking about going on dates and stuff. But all they do is make noise and keep us from practicing."

"Why do you think they were sniffing the Dust-Off?"

"Because they're stupid. All they want to do is get high and stuff. That's nasty." He shudders in revulsion.

His reaction to the nasty girls isn't out of character. Michael's fear and distrust of women is palpable. Apart from Tracy and my mom, he can't bring himself to say two words to any female, and it took a lot of gentle cajoling to get him to warm up to them. If he were younger, I'd say he thought they had cooties—and any contact would contaminate him.

It doesn't take a therapist to recognize his fear is a reaction to his mom. Every couple of months, just like clockwork, he'll mention how angry he is with her. We're relieved he can express those feelings instead of letting them fester. But he's not willing to explore them any further. Until he's ready to look at it, there's little we can do, other than bring women into his life who can help him see that not every woman will hurt him deeply.

After we talk, Michael runs off to play with his brothers, but the situation stays with me. I sit at my desk, staring at my work, not ready to pick it up again. It takes me a long time to recognize I am furious.

If I saw those girls on the street, I'd want to knock their heads together. I'm pissed they exposed my son to substance abuse again. I know my reaction is completely irrational and immature, and I know I'm being overprotective and juvenile at the same time. He managed to survive ten years with a drug-addicted mother, and the addle-brained antics of some gawky girls aren't going to be the tipping point.

So I try to sit with my anger and understand what is behind it. Slowly, the answer comes. I'm afraid. Studies show that 70 percent of kids with addicted parents wind up being addicts themselves; and I fret, worried any new exposure might prove to be the first step on that long, dark road. Little Michael may be afraid of drugs now, but what would happen if the curiosity became stronger than his own fear? There'd be absolutely nothing I could do to stop him.

I used to wonder how my parents, who were part of the young, liberal generation that voted John Kennedy into office, grew into the ultraconservatives they are today. Dad and I haven't talked politics since he voted for Ronald Reagan in 1980. It's just too inflammatory.

Back then, when I was just graduating from college and certain I knew everything, we'd have blazing arguments in which I would taunt him, insulting a conservativism I couldn't comprehend. I was just a snot. My poor father's lips would turn white, but he would just absorb the insults and say quietly, "When you're older, you'll understand."

Now, it's scary to realize I actually do. There's something about parenthood that inherently drives you to become more conservative. It's all about a desire to protect your children from the vices you once embraced, or to keep them from experimenting with the ones you were too afraid to try. In a world full of scary things, you'll do anything to protect your children.

When I find myself clucking like a disapproving chicken, or the word no pops out of my mouth without thinking, I know I'm in trouble. I need to stop and reconsider what I'm saying and doing. No child thrives in a world of fear and control, and that is not the world I want to create for my children.

One of the big lessons we had to learn going through the process of adoption was that once we set the intention, we had to trust things would work out as they should. If we couldn't do that, we'd drive ourselves—and everyone else—crazy.

Just like my parents couldn't control the world they brought me into, I can't control the world my sons live in; just like my parents tried to give me the values I would need to make my way, I've got to do the same; and just like my parents had to accept that they couldn't prevent me from making mistakes, I've got to trust that our intention for our boys will become their reality.

It's a freeing moment when I realize I have to let go. I can't control whether Michael will ever deal with his anger or ever decide to try drugs. What I can do is help to give him the tools he needs to make his way. There might be a world of nasty girls out there, but I know Michael's going to be just fine.

## Taking Personal Inventory

There's a new boy in Dereck's fourth grade class, and for weeks, Dereck's been asking to have a sleepover. I tell him it's fine to invite Chris on Friday, when the school closes at noon for a teacher's workshop.

Dereck calls immediately, and while they're on the phone, I say, "Remind Chris his mom will have to let the school know it's okay for us to pick him up." Standing in the kitchen making dinner, I hear Chris yell to his mom and her yelling back that she'll take care of it.

On Friday, I pick up our boys and Chris, and we all go out to Mel's Diner for lunch; five chocolate milk shakes and five orders of chili cheese fries later, the boys are sated and ready to play. We load the dogs into the minivan and head to the dog park, where the dogs can roam, the older boys can play football, and Matthew can play on the swing set and jungle gym.

"This is really cool," Chris tells me. "We never take our dog to the park." Later, all the boys decide they want to see a movie, and I ask Chris to phone his mom to see if that's okay. He calls, she says yes, and so we take them to the theater.

Later, sitting around the dinner table, Chris tells us about his family. He lives with his mom and his older brother, and he only sees his dad on weekends. He went to a Catholic school last year, loves the Schoolhouse, and has a crush on Lupita, a girl in their class.

He beams at the attention. Dereck just rolls his eyes. "My dads always ask us a lot of questions," he says. "They're really nosey."

When Chris' mom picks him up on Saturday, Daddy Michael answers the door. I can hear them talking as I come up the stairs. When she sees me, she looks startled, her eyes darting back and forth between us. She masks her discomfort quickly, but there's no question. She had no idea Dereck had two dads.

We chat for a minute, fill her in on everything the boys did, and tell her Chris was great to have around. "He likes to eat, and any kid who eats is always welcome at our house," I tell her. She smiles, murmurs her thanks, and whisks him out the door.

Chris turns around as they're walking toward the driveway and calls out, "Thanks again! I had fun!"

"I wonder if that's the last time Chris will hang out here," I ask Daddy Michael as we close the door.

Michael's always the optimist. "I don't think it bothered her too much. Why would she put her kids in a school with so many diverse families if it did?"

"You saw the look on her face. It said it all."

"We've got to give her a chance. I'm sure she'll come around."

"I don't know." We've been remarkably fortunate. This is actually the first time we've experienced even a whiff of discomfort about our family, and I'm as sensitive as a seismograph. The faintest rumbling sets me aquiver.

The following Monday, we host a fund-raising event for the boys' school at our house. A bunch of other parents come to hear about a planned campus expansion, and one of the moms grabs me in the kitchen after, unable to suppress her curiosity.

"You guys are so wonderful to take in three brothers like that! That's so amazing! Was it hard?" I smile graciously, and she races on. "Tell me. Your oldest. How did he handle having two dads? Wasn't it too weird for him, you know, just starting puberty and everything?"

My jaw drops a bit, and just as I'm about to respond, her husband tugs on her sleeve and reminds her they need to get home. They say their good-byes, and she makes a point to hug me. I walk them to the door, still smiling, but underneath, I'm fuming. We've just hit a 7.9 on my Richter scale.

I'm not sure why both moms get under my skin so. From the moment I came out, I've experienced countless sideways glances and awkward lulls in conversation. I keenly feel the reality that there are certain rights my straight brethren take for granted but that I may not see in my lifetime.

Michael and I can't marry; we had to spend thousands of dollars in legal fees to make sure each of us is protected in case something happens to the other. We can't imagine ever wanting to, but we know we can't drive through Oklahoma without the risk that a crazy cop might take our kids from us. We know the oblique reference to activist judges and the knowing smirk during the president's 2006 State of the Union address are one more slam at people like us.

But it feels different when it happens in my own home.

Reading Doris Kearns Goodwin's new biography of Lincoln the night before, I was struck by a quote from Frederick Douglass. Douglass said Lincoln was "the first great man that I talked with in the United

States freely, who in no single instance reminded me of the difference between himself and myself."

And that's the crux of it right there. I don't want to be reminded we are different.

Of course we are. But we are just as different from Chris's divorced mom and dad as we are from Jeff and Wade, Mike and Steve, Patrick and Matt, George and Tod, and Geoff and David, or any of the other gay parents at our school. And that's the whole point—I don't want to serve as someone's comfortable stereotype, especially standing in my own kitchen.

When everyone else leaves the house and we start cleaning up, I recount the mom's comments to Daddy Michael. I get so mad again, I find myself slamming cupboard doors. Michael shushes me like a baby. "Come on, you're going to wake up Matthew. She meant well. And if you'd had a moment, I know you would have straightened her out."

He tries to change the subject. "By the way, did you hear what that other dad said during the meeting?"

"You mean Dave?" He nods, and I find myself stopping short. Dave had ambled into the house like a former football player: big, strapping, and casual. He wore work boots, a plaid flannel shirt, and a scruffy beard. Immediately, I wrote him off as a numbskull former jock. My opinion was confirmed when Dereck, who is usually shy, walked right up to him and said, "I know you. You're Lily's dad. You threw us the football in the playground."

But my first read on Dave was completely off the mark; he was warm and gracious and played with the dogs and asked lots of questions about the home renovations we'd done. There was a sweet gentleness when he talked about his children and why he and his wife sent them to this school even though it was a real financial stretch. "I want them to be color-blind, in every sense of the word."

Every parent in our living room had nodded in agreement when Dave spoke.

Remembering Dave's words—and my initial judgment of him, I hang my head. I was so busy getting worked up about the splinter in that mom's eye, I couldn't see the log in my own.

Embarrassed, I tell Michael, "I guess I have take my own inventory before I can judge anyone else."

He raises an eyebrow, trying to be solemn. "Be the change you want to see," he intones.

We both burst out laughing. "Alright, already. I get it." And thank goodness, I really do.

# The Letter, Part I

When I pick up Dereck at his friend Giacomo's on Saturday morning, Jennifer warns me. "Dereck might get a little crabby today. They were up playing and didn't get a lot of sleep last night. And of course, neither did I." She pulls her Jackie-O sunglasses down just long enough to reveal the dark circles under her eyes. "Gone are the days I could be up all night and look fresh as a daisy in the morning!"

Dereck's quiet and a little sleepy-eyed in the car heading home, but when he gets home, his mood turns dark. We're all doing chores around the house, so Daddy Michael asks him to power hose the deck. Dereck balks. "I don't feel like it," he says.

Michael insists, pointing out there's a lot of yard work to do, and everyone else is working. Grumbling, Dereck says, "Alright." He heads outside, but comes back just a few minutes later. "I'm done," he says. "Can I play now?"

It's not a quick chore, so Michael is skeptical. He and Dereck go out to inspect his work, and sure enough, it's not been done. It looks like Dereck splashed a little water around and turned on his heel.

"Dereck, are you sure you power hosed the deck?"

"Yes."

"Then why is the power hose still up against the wall where I left it?"

"I used it."

"Dereck, there's no way you could have. There's still cobwebs on the handle."

"I did! God, why can't you believe me?"

"Dereck, the power hose hasn't even been moved. Do you want to tell me the truth?"

Dereck's face turns beet red, but he won't back down.

Finally, Michael, exasperated, sends him to his room. Dereck stomps by me as I work in the kitchen and slams his door with a flourish.

"What the hell was that?" I ask Michael as he walks toward me, shaking his head.

"I don't get it. There's no reason for him to lie. What is wrong with him?"

"I know he's tired. But that's no excuse. Let him stew a while, and I'll go talk to him."

I wait a full forty-five minutes, thinking that may give him time to reconsider. He's sitting on his bed, face still flushed, lower lip jutting out dangerously. I often tease him that his lip is a barometer of his mood—the more it sticks out, the madder he is.

But he's clearly not up for light banter today. "So Dereck, do you want to talk about what's going on?"

It's the invitation he's been waiting for. He leaps up dramatically, and tears spring from his eyes. "I miss my mom! I want my mom!" He throws himself on the floor, his skinny body wracked with sobs, making all the burbling noises that come whenever he tantrums.

Little Michael and Matthew, both outside doing chores, hear him, and I see them stop and look up at the bedroom window. Little Michael just shakes his head and goes back to his work. He doesn't have a lot of patience for Dereck's theatrics, either.

Dereck has at it for at least twenty minutes, wailing. He reaches for me and wraps his arms around my waist, sobbing into my T-shirt, while I murmur some comfort.

As I hold him, I feel oddly detached. The first time he exploded like this, I was horrified and alarmed, worried we weren't doing something we needed to do to take care of him. Now there's a part of me that feels he does it deliberately, just for attention. Of all the boys, he is the most in control, no matter how out of control he seems. It's like he watches himself with one eye, always calculating the impact of his behavior.

Today's cycle is no different than ones we've seen before; I've caught on to the rhythm of his outbursts. When he starts making big, gulping "boo hoo" noises, I know he's running out of steam. He'll be ready to talk in a moment.

I wait until he's calmed down. "Dereck, there are two things we have to talk about here. I'm sorry you are really missing your mother, but you know it is no excuse for lying to Daddy Michael. Why did you lie?"

"I didn't want to do it, and I knew Daddy Michael would get mad if I said no."

"Dereck, you know Daddy Michael is reasonable. He knew you were up late last night at Giacomo's. What do you think he would have said if you told him you were tired and offered to do it later?"

He thought for a moment. "He probably would have said okay."

"You're right. So why did you lie?"

"I dunno. I guess I should apologize."

"Yes, you should. And there're probably going to be consequences for lying. You know lying is about the worst thing you can do in this house."

He looks down and nods his head.

"So let's talk about what you said about your mom. We've talked about this before, but I'm not sure it's something you understand. I know how much you love her, and I'm really sorry you can't live with her. Even though she loves you very much, she's not able to take care of you."

He looks up to me, eyes puffy and swollen. His lower lip juts out dangerously again, and I can almost read what is going through his mind. "Dereck, is it hard for you to believe that your mom can't care of you?"

He shakes his head and begins to sob again. In his mind, his mom is perfect, and there is no way she is not able to care for him. There is no way she could have let him go, even though that is precisely what happened. He clings to his belief like a shield, trying to hold the pain of separation at bay.

I realize this outburst, like all the ones before it, helps him release the tension between what he wishes were true and the reality he can't allow himself to acknowledge. He is acting out his dissonance, hoping against hope that we can help him figure out a way to bridge the gap.

So we talk again about disease and addiction, how it can make people do things they might not otherwise do. "I know my mom's brain is messed up," he tells me. "Like those pictures in *Time* magazine of people's brains who used drugs."

Slowly, slowly, he is taking baby steps toward acknowledging his mother's addiction. And he is learning that to acknowledge the truth doesn't mean he has to lay blame. He can love his mother and hate her addiction. He can love his mother and mourn the dissolution of his family. He can love his mother, and find space in his heart to love his new dads.

Finally, he is calm and ready to make amends. "I'll go tell Daddy Michael I'm sorry," he says. "And then I'll really clean the deck." He hugs me one more time and runs out of his room.

I sit on his bed for a moment, exhausted by the fever pitch of his emotion. He's the most amazingly sensitive boy. Perhaps his awareness of his own pain is what makes him acutely sensitive to the pain of others.

I suspect that this outburst is an unconscious reaction to his mother's emotional upheaval—just days earlier, his mother once again tried to make contact with the boys. Every time she does this, Dereck senses it and winds up having an outburst like this one, crying and calling for his mother. He'd been disconsolate for three days the first time she'd approached the social worker begging to see the boys; we offered to set up the post office box then. He had no clue she'd make contact, but somehow, he had felt her energy.

His last outburst had been three weeks ago, just as his mother had called the social worker to ask if we would set up the post office box again. She had never followed through and written to the boys, so we'd just allowed it to lapse. When the social worker called again, we told her we would open it for three months more. If she didn't use it during that time, we would not open it again.

We didn't tell the boys, not wanting to get their hopes up. But somehow, some way, Dereck had sensed she was trying to connect, and it had triggered an emotional upheaval just like the one today.

Now I realized again that Dereck, on some profoundly psychic level, is aware of what she is doing. It doesn't take long to confirm that feeling. The social worker calls on Monday morning to tell me to check the post office box. Just around the time Dereck had begun to wail on Saturday, his birth mom was leaving a message for the social worker, anxious to make sure they would get the letter she had just mailed.

Hanging up the phone, I shake my head in wonder. There's nothing like the connection between a mother and her son.

## The Letter, Part II

When I pick up birth mom's letter at the post office box, I decide to read it before showing it to the boys. What I read makes me weep.

It's been nineteen months since the boys last heard from her. Now I hold her letter in my hands, two thin sheets with yellow and purple violets around the bottom border, written in a childish hand that looks like one of Matthew's homework assignments.

We'd told her she could write more than a year ago, but now, holding the letter in my hand, I tremble. What Pandora's box are we opening?

Her anguish is apparent from the first lines.

> *I love you boys with all my heart and miss you so very much!! You need to believe this. There is not a day that goes by that I don't think of you! I feel so lost without my sons.*

She shares about her life, and I know what she says will hurt and worry them. She's moved to Colorado to live near her sister, which is a good thing. But her boyfriend, the one who had beaten and abused her, has followed her there—a horrifying thing. She tells the boys how wonderful he is and how she wishes they had gotten to know him. I know how they will react to that; he scared the daylights out of them the only time they met.

She seems confused.

> *Let me guess please correct me if I'm wrong Michael you are 14 years old, Dereck you are 11 years old, Mat-Mat you are 7 years old.*

Has she really forgotten how old her sons are? Maybe that explains why the post office box remained empty around each of their birthdays.

She concludes by telling the boys,

*You are so lucky to have the parents you do. You deserve
the best in life please tell your parents thank you so very
much.*

Is she willing to acknowledge they have a better life now, or is this
a way to ingratiate herself with us?

I read the letter over and over, wondering if and how we can share
it with all three boys. Michael is away on a photo shoot. When I read
it over the phone to him, he cries, too, and he wonders the same thing.
We agree we will share the contents of the letter with the boys, in
whatever way we finally decide is best, when he gets back. We need
those extra days to think about the best way to handle it, and we know
it will take both of us to handle the reactions, whatever they may be.

I realize I need some advice, so I call my mother. Her reaction is
swift, a mother hen protecting her extended brood. "Don't let that
bitch burrow her way in again. She had her chance to be their mother,
and she walked away. Keep her away from those kids!"

"Wow, Mom. I wasn't expecting you to be so adamant."

"Don't ask, then, if you don't want to know what I think."

"I didn't mean that. You know how much Dereck misses her. I
don't want him or any of them coming back later to accuse us of not
allowing them to have contact with her."

"She's just being manipulative. You've worked too hard getting
them to a place where they feel safe and stable. This is just going to
mess with them."

"Maybe, but think of it this way. Reading the letter could be
like an inoculation. It will build some immunity if they have a little
exposure."

"Well, I wouldn't put those boys through that, but I'm not their
parent. Let her stay in Colorado."

Michael and I have decided to wait until Saturday to talk to the
boys, so we can be with them all day. On Friday night, Michael and I go
to dinner with our friends Belinda and Thane, while their son Harrison
and Little Michael, both fourteen, baby-sit the younger boys.

Over margaritas, Belinda jumps on my mother's bandwagon. "I'm
sorry. She's just going to suck the life right out of Dereck if you don't
figure out a way to protect him. Michael's old enough to handle it.

Dereck's just a little boy, and don't even think about sharing anything with Matthew!"

Michael's taken aback. "But we should be honest with them, shouldn't we?"

Belinda softens a bit and puts her hand on Michael's arm. "Dereck is only eleven years old. You can't treat him like an adult. You're responsible to protect him. It's really okay to edit out the things that could hurt him. That's what parents do. He just wants to know his mom is okay and that she thinks of him. Leave the rest out."

Michael still looks anguished. "I just know the boys have a spiritual connection to their mother. If we tamper with that, we're doing them harm. Even if she's a mess, she gave birth to them."

Belinda has a sudden revelation. "You know what, Michael? It's a spiritual connection, but it's been broken because the birth mom is broken. Kids learn how to love from their mothers, and what you really want is for Dereck to continue to develop his own capacity to love. That's what your intention should be—that he can overcome how he was hurt and grow into a fully loving man. Set the intention for his healing from that broken relationship. Then he will heal—and I bet in some way, it would help to heal his mother, too."

Michael listens and then looks at me. When I nod, he says, "Yes, we can do that."

Silently, I mouth a "thank you" across the table. She's given Michael an approach that lets him feel less guilty, and one we can both live with.

The next day, I ask Little Michael if we can talk to him in our office. "Am I in trouble?"

"Not at all. There's something we need to ask your opinion about."

We close the door, and he looks alarmed and confused. "What did I do?"

"Nothing, honey." I explain about the letter and that there are things that might hurt Dereck and Matthew in it. "We know you're mature enough to handle it, but we're not sure how they will react. Would you read the letter and tell us what you think?"

He nods, suddenly very severe and grown-up. Chewing his lip, he reads slowly. He looks up after he gets through the first page. "At least she's working," he says, and then pauses to look at me. "At least she's trying to be responsible."

I bite my lip and look back at him. Learning to be responsible has been my mantra to him over the past few months, and in a flash I know how much shame I've brought my son. Every admonition has been a reminder that he is like the woman who has hurt him so deeply.

But he looks again at me, wise beyond his years, and shakes his head slightly, telling me it's okay. "Dereck isn't ready to read this. Let me talk to him. That way he won't think you're trying to keep something from him, and he won't get upset."

"You can all write her if you want to. Is that something you'd like to do?"

With a shrug of his thin shoulders, he's all kid again. "I dunno." He's had enough. He hands the letter back to me and hugs us both. "Maybe I'll talk to Dereck tomorrow."

Little Michael doesn't mention the letter to Dereck at all the next day, and I know he, too, is afraid of the reaction. So while the two of them are playing with the dogs on the floor in our office, we tell Dereck we've heard from his mom.

His reaction is decidedly low-key. He moves to the chair in the corner and pulls his knees up to his chin. He listens as we share that she's living in Colorado and that she says she misses them terribly. He shows nothing on his usually expressive face. He doesn't ask for any more details; he doesn't ask any questions at all.

"How do you feel right now?" I ask.

He thinks for a moment and says, "Okay." I can tell he means it. When I ask him if he wants to write to her, he shrugs his shoulders, his response noncommittal. Dereck has kept alive his fantasy mom because he couldn't face the truth of his real mom and her addiction. Nineteen months after he saw her last, this concrete information has gently burst his bubble. He slowly absorbs the change.

Quietly, and with more grace than I could ever expect, Dereck begins to let go. It's a rite of passage, and in that moment, he takes one more step from childhood to young manhood. There is a new soberness in his face that wasn't there minutes before, and I am both sad for him and proud of him.

Our sons know they have to respond to the letter, but they seem almost reluctant to do it. Dereck finally asks me to write to tell their mom how they are doing. "We'll write something on the bottom of the letter," he says, and that's what the three boys do.

Michael scrawls, "Hi, Mom. Happy Valentine's Day! Michael." Matthew tells her he loves her, taking great care to print his name clearly. When it is his turn, Dereck reads over the letter and writes quickly, "Just to let you know, Mom, I love you, and I pray for you every night. Dereck."

When he's finished, he gets up from the desk and starts to leave the room. But he stops and turns, saying, "Daddy John, can we go to Target? I need to get a new binder for school." Grabbing my car keys, I know he's definitely moved on.

## Far From Home

It's a humid night on the Yucatan Peninsula, and I toss and turn in my little hut, cramped on a bed that is too small for my frame.

I don't want to be here. My friends, Belinda and Gahl, talked me into spending my birthday week at this yoga retreat, and after a quick phone call from Belinda, Michael offered the trip as a birthday gift.

I felt pressured to go, but when I nearly missed the flight out from Los Angeles, I almost turned around and drove back home. I couldn't shake a strange sense of dread, even though Michael insisted I deserved five days of quiet to write and meditate.

Before bed tonight, I spent a twenty-dollar phone card speaking with Michael, who talked nonstop about how irritable and irritating the boys had been today. He told me he said to them, "Would you act like this for Daddy John?" Their immediate silence gave the answer.

"I can't wait for them to go to school tomorrow." His voice trailed off for a moment, and I tried to make suggestions about what might get the boys back on track. But he didn't hear me; he'd been saving up for this call, and once he took a breath, he started in again, talking fast, his frustration pouring out. All I could do was listen.

I finally had to interrupt him to tell him the phone card was about to run out and the store was closed, so I couldn't buy another. We quickly said good night, murmuring "I love you" just as the line went dead. I walked back to my little hut, my mind thousands of miles away.

Even now as I lay in bed, I can picture Michael sitting at his desk in the office, the television mounted on the wall above his head, the volume up loud. I can see little Michael and Dereck shouting as they play Xbox in Michael's room. I know exactly where the dogs are lying and just how Matthew's head is tucked against his pillow as he sleeps.

It's my job to keep track. I am Daddy John, the enforcer—the parent who makes the boys use their napkins and do their homework and brush their teeth. But in the rare times I am not there, the boys test the limits, pushing and prodding and challenging Michael until he sputters with fatigue, worn thin and weary.

Lying in my short, uncomfortable bed, I barely notice the calming ocean waves outside. I feel guilty and frustrated. "Damn it," I yell at the moon. "Why can't I get a break? Why do I have to worry that Little Michael isn't brushing his teeth?"

That's exactly why I agreed to come here, albeit kicking and screaming. I'm not sure I like what I've become, and I don't know what I need to do to change. Before the boys came to us last year, I had a career—a real career—with outlandish hours and travel and public visibility. I went to work each day feeling confident, sure of who I was because of what I did.

When the boys came, I knew I had to cut back; I couldn't manage eighty-hour workweeks on two coasts with three boys who needed to learn to trust their new dads. I left my job, hoping to find enough freelance work to pay the bills.

I've been blessed—the work has come and the boys have thrived. After years of upheaval, they are relieved to have some structure and consistency. They can relax and be children again.

Their happiness makes me happy. But despite this, there's a gnawing sense of incompleteness. Every time someone asks what I do, I find the answer sticking in my throat. Just what am I? A househusband? A stay-at-home dad? A consultant who only cares to work enough to get by? The question makes me feel isolated and disconnected.

All my markers have changed. At forty-seven, I feel extraordinarily blessed in life. I love Michael. I love my children. But there is still some fragment of my heart that is starved in all this abundance; I feel like an anachronistic blur, the link you click on your computer screen that gets you to someplace else. I am just a conduit, passing on life without experiencing it myself.

Here in Tulum, I find it difficult to interact with my fellow yogis. I take little notice of the sun and the waves and beautiful sky. My mind is stuck at home, and I don't have the energy to extend myself to new people.

Belinda and Gahl are also here for quiet space to write. Belinda's on deadline for a screenplay, and Gahl is struggling with the last chapters of his second book. We form a little insular group, spending our free time sitting around a table, sipping tea and facing our laptops. The hours pass with each absorbed in our own screen, writing as catharsis and as a means of escape.

On Wednesday morning, I wake up feeling something in the air that matches the gloom in my heart. We plan to skip some sessions and head to a place where we can swim with dolphins, and we stop at the front desk on our way out. There's a little notice taped on the counter, showing the approach of an epic hurricane, poised in the ocean and headed straight for the coastline where we stand.

Belinda takes one look at the notice and says, "I'm sorry, boys, but I'm out of here." In a flash, she's on the phone, changing her flight home. She comes back to us, saying, "Get out now. That's all I'm going to say." In what seems like moments, she's packed and checked out, loading her bags into a taxi for the two-hour ride to the airport. She kisses us and says again, "I'm not kidding. My intuition tells me this will be bad. Go. Now."

I buy another phone card and call Michael, asking if he's heard anything about a hurricane heading toward Yucatan. "No, but let me check the news. Call me back in a few minutes."

When I do, his voice sounds different. "It's a category five. It's supposed to hit tomorrow. CNN says it's stronger than Katrina. They're going to close the airport. You've got to get to higher ground. How quickly can you leave?"

I call the airline, trying to get on a flight today; there's nothing available, and they tell me to check in at the airport in case something should open up. They won't confirm the airport is closing, but the woman does say, "If I were you, I'd try to get out today."

Suddenly, I realize everyone else on the retreat is doing the same thing. A woman from Phoenix is talking to her husband on a cell phone—I can hear him screaming, "Get the fuck out. Now!" The woman and her friend, who has been listening in on the conversation, begin to shake and cry, and it sets everyone into a panic. One by one, our retreat leaders drive away, leaving a group of confused folks, all making solitary decisions about what to do.

Gahl is a tough Israeli who believes he was a warrior in past lives; he's ready for a new adventure and decides to drive inland to experience the storm. I think of my kids, and all I want to do is get home. When I walk back to my hut to pack, the ocean is already lapping against the door; the room will flood if the waves get any higher. I pack quickly and go back to the front desk. Two women from New York are loading their things into a taxi, and I ask if I can hitch a ride. "Of course. Get in."

In an instant, we're on our way, and the tiny isthmus where we stayed fades away; closer to the airport, my cell service works, and I can call Michael. "The airport is still open," he says. "I tried to get you on a waiting list, but they're not taking any names. Do you have money and water?" The rain is pelting against the taxi, and periodically, the wind catches under the wheels and shakes the car. Each time we hydroplane, the women with me turn white. The funny thing is, the crazier things get, the calmer I become.

At the airport, it's pure pandemonium. Every tourist has turned into an ugly American. They push and jostle in the lines, screaming obscenities and trying to intimidate frightened airline personnel into making miracles. Every time the automatic doors open, the wind blows in, sending paper and trash and a howling rain through the lines.

After two and a half hours, I reach the counter. I smile and speak gently; the poor woman doesn't need one more American shouting at her. "There's nothing left tonight," she says. "I'm so sorry. But I hear they may bring in additional planes in the morning, before they close the airport. They'll try to get out as many people as they can. So come back early. I've priority wait-listed you. That's the best I can do." She actually pats my hand as she hands back my ticket.

"Thank you," I tell her. "Be safe." She gives me a wan smile.

I don't want to stay at the airport overnight, so I decide to take a shuttle into Cancun to find a hotel; they'll definitely have rooms available. Walking past the airport bar, I see two other women from our retreat at a table, both sobbing. When I stop, they jump up and throw their arms around me. "We can't get out until tomorrow morning and we don't have any cash and we don't want to stay here …"

I tell them to come with me; we'll find a place to stay, and I'll spring for dinner. The shuttle drives through the rain past all the big resort hotels on the beach. None will accept another guest tonight. The driver finally deposits us in front of a small local inn that will give us a room. We arrange for a taxi back to the airport at five in the morning and set off in the blinding rain to find dinner.

We laugh and giggle and share secrets over dinner, refugees who have nothing to hide. After burritos and three margaritas apiece, we're feeling no pain, so we head to the hotel.

When I call home, Matthew answers. "Daddy John, are you in the hurricane? Is it going to be like Katrina?" He starts to cry.

"I'm doing my best to get home tomorrow, but even if I have to stay, I'll be fine. I'm ready."

"But I want you to come home."

"I'll do my best. You can say a prayer for me, okay?"

"Okay. I love you, Daddy John."

"I love you, too."

All night, workers nail plywood over the hotel windows. That noise and the howling wind make sleep impossible. At five the next morning, we head back to the airport; the driver curses over and over at flooded roads, making detour after detour until we finally arrive.

The airport itself looks like a disaster zone. Trash and debris cover every spot not taken up by the hordes of sleeping tourists waiting to get out. I say a quick good-bye to my new friends and get into a line.

It snakes slowly up to the counter, and the mood is even uglier than yesterday. Real fear has crept into the lines, and the constant pushing and shoving is dark and mean. I wait for nearly three hours for my turn. I hand over my ticket and ask about earlier flights. The weary woman behind the counter types into her computer and glances up at me.

"You're strong," she says. I nod at her, not quite sure what she means. "And you've just got carry-on, right?" I nod again. She looks around quickly and whispers conspiratorially, "Run. Now." Her head jerks to her left, towards airport security. "Go through there and get to Gate B5 as quick as you can. The plane is leaving in a few minutes. It's the last one out. If you get to the gate, you'll have the last seat. I'll call ahead to tell them you're on your way."

I thank her and do as she says, running as fast as I can through the crowds. The gate is a long way away, and I can hear them calling my name as I approach. I wave, trying to get their attention. They wave back sharply, urging me to hurry. I reach the gate; the agent checks my passport and waves me on. "Quick. They're going to close the doors."

I race on board, and make my way down the aisle to the back of the plane. The ticket agent was right. I have the last seat. I can hear the pilot telling the passengers they are lucky—we're the last flight out before the airport closes. As I sit down, I see the anxious flight attendants nod, and soon, we're taking off.

Around me, children continue to cry, and unhappy adults, angry their vacations have been cut short, are muttering that Cancun is nothing but a third-rate, Third World destination. I hear the fear behind their anger. These moms and dads have just escaped something potentially terrible; it's a way to release their horror without falling apart.

It's only after we're in the air that I begin to realize how I've been blessed. There are thousands of people just like me in that airport, waiting out a hurricane that will trap them without food and water and electricity for days. Somehow, for some reason, my fate is different. Somehow, for some reason, I get to go home.

My boys are waiting for me, and I can't help but believe it's the power of their desire to bring me home that has guided my way. I murmur a quiet "thank-you" and settle back into my seat.

Slowly, the ennui that had enveloped me all week fades away, and a quiet gratitude fills the space it has left behind. I'm blessed to be heading back to the place where I belong, and in a way I could not have realized the day before, there is no place I would rather be.

## The Rage Within

Matthew got into a fight today. He and his classmate Jacob went at it at Gaia's eighth birthday party, when they banged into each other on the jumper. Jacob called Matthew a "retard," and within seconds, Matthew had his hands around Jacob's throat, choking him. A few body blows from each kid, and they rolled off the jumper. Quick as a flash, the fight was over.

Matthew wouldn't have said anything about it, of course, except that one of the parents chaperoning made a smug reference to the "incident" when we were picking him up. It's the second time in two weeks Matthew has gotten into a fight with a classmate, and we're fit to be tied, trying to figure out what to do.

He sits in our office, skinny arms folded across his chest, bright pink spots covering the freckles on his round cheeks. "Alright, young man, tell me what happened."

"He called me a retard and told me I was stupid."

"But why did you choke him, Matthew?"

"Because I wanted him to stop."

"Matthew, what did we tell you to do when someone was bothering you?"

"Go find an adult and ask for help."

"And why didn't you?"

"Eduardo's dad was right there, and he heard me say stop, but he didn't do anything. And Eduardo kept telling Jacob to fight." The pink spots on Matthew's checks get decidedly redder, and everything begins to fall into place. Matthew must have felt like a trapped animal.

Jacob, the boy Matthew fought with, is best friends with Eduardo, and they often gang up on the other kids. His dad, Jerry, adopted him as a single parent; and Jerry's new partner constantly complains that the kid acts sweet on the surface, but underneath, he's a little snake. He tells everyone that Jerry allows the nanny to feed Eduardo his dinner in the bathtub. Eduardo's a very spoiled boy indeed.

Since Jerry is convinced his son can do no wrong, there's no way he would think to intercede. And he was the smug one who couldn't wait to tell us of the incident between the boys.

I find myself burning with anger, too. That Jerry is a wormy little fucker. No wonder Matthew couldn't figure out what to do. Matthew's watching me intently as I try to calm down. "If you're in a situation where an adult isn't going to help you, the best thing you can do is just walk away."

"But what if I want to play?"

"It's better to walk away and find someone else to play with."

"Okay."

"Matthew, I'm most concerned that you decided to choke Jacob. Especially after we had the conversation last week about fighting."

"But he called me a retard, and I didn't like it."

"Do you think that he deserved to be hit for saying that?"

"No." He starts to fidget. He knows he's responsible for having gotten into the fight, but I can tell there's something more.

"Something else is bothering you, Matthew, I can tell. What is it?"

"I don't like it when you and Daddy Michael fight."

"But we don't hit each other."

"But you yell. Like you did this morning."

And there's the thunderbolt. I'd blown up at Michael this morning, and even though we argued behind the closed door of our office, I know the boys were all listening on the stairs just outside. Matthew, upset by what he'd heard, had carried it with him the rest of the day.

The problem isn't Matthew; it's me. The realization brings tears to my eyes. This is the last thing I want my children to see. My anger has always been my dirty little secret—the one that people who don't know me well proclaim surprise when I admit to.

As a child, I was terrified to watch my grandparents scream and throw dishes into the street, and I vowed I would never let myself lose control like that.

No inflammatory blow-ups for me; no flying pots and pans, no plates of pasta sailing across West Sixty-first Street. Instead, I shaped my anger into something cold and steely, turned on and off like a faucet. No matter how white hot, no matter how enraged, my will was stronger. Anger was something to be controlled and tamped down, the wild and riotous thing that must be tamed at all costs.

That all changed when I was with my second partner, Eric. He was the rebound I'd latched onto after my first, fourteen-year relationship ended. The attraction was purely physical, but in every other way, we were oil and water. It didn't take long after we'd moved from Michigan to California to make us both wish we'd never met.

Miserable in his new job, miserable away from his family, miserable he couldn't do drugs and party without recrimination, Eric took to goading me, needling, and taunting to exploit our common misery. For months, I would just climb into bed and cry, horrified I'd made such a mistake and wondering how I could live with myself after two failed relationships.

I finally hit a breaking point on the last night of a particularly miserable three-day weekend. Eric had been pushing for a fight all day, and I'd retreated to a spare bedroom just to get away. He couldn't stand being ignored, and he burst in, grabbing the book I was reading from my hands and throwing it against the wall.

The desecration of the book did me in. Before I was conscious of what I was doing, I'd leapt from the bed, lifted him with one hand over my head and thrown him to the ground. I could feel myself punching him and screaming, "Don't you ever do that to me again!"

When it was over, I sat on the bed, breathing hard and in shock. I had never hit anyone in my life, and I had never lost control in the way I just had. I'd just discovered my breaking point—and how easily I could turn into the very thing that repulsed me.

What was just as horrifying was that Eric actually liked it; he lay on the floor with a glint in his eye I'd never seen before, and for the few months we still lived in the same house, he continued to push and prod, trying to provoke me, hungry and eager for another brutal altercation.

The next few months were a painful blur of therapy and new beginnings. I was horrified to know I could behave this way, horrified at the sick and twisted turn my life had taken, horrified that the absolutes which had always defined my conduct began to crumble. It was all I could do to struggle to regain control of the rage that had bubbled out of me. It was the monster in the dark, the thing I was most afraid of, and even though I knew I must get to its source, I couldn't bear the risk involved. So I shut the door firmly, and added lock after lock, hoping it would be contained.

But no emotion, no matter how tightly bound, can remain subterranean for good. It has a way of seeping out, like cracks along a fault line, until some cataclysmic trigger gives it full reign to burst forth again. And so when Matthew looks at me, with all his childlike innocence and hunger to emulate, I realize I am a walking powder keg, with a slowly burning fuse attached. It is only a matter of time before I blow again.

My tears pour out, and Matthew, perplexed, comes toward me and rubs his hands along the sides of my head. "Don't cry, Daddy John. I'll do better next time."

"I'm not crying about you, Matthew. I'm crying about me. I'm sorry I couldn't control myself better this morning. I shouldn't have yelled."

"That's okay, Daddy John. I know you didn't mean to be mean to Daddy Michael."

It may seem simplistic to say my child hits because he sees that impulse in me, but I've learned full well that our children are our mirrors. And if I want to see him learn to deal with the anger that leads him to strike out, I am going to have to plumb the depths of my own dark heart. The prospect scares me to my core, but I know I must do this, not just for myself, but also for the child who looks to me to learn how to live.

## The Basketball Grouch

I am a big, fat grouch.

It's no small satisfaction that I am the tallest, the strongest, and the meanest bully in the household. I can make the rest of the crew jump to it whenever I raise my voice. And I'm the one who makes them nervous and edgy, wondering why I have to bluster and rant, certain I can get my way by shouting, intimidating, and overpowering the weaker, smaller voices around me.

I'm not happy with what I am. As we sit on the plane, heading to Hawaii on the boys' second visit to Uncle Richard and Aunt Suzanne, there are a few blissful moments of quiet, but I don't enjoy them. Instead, I find myself reflecting on the monster that is me. We're in the middle of their two-week Easter break, and the past five days have been unadulterated chaos.

There's a whiff of spring testosterone in the air, with the boys becoming baseball maniacs, screaming and shouting as they throw baseball after baseball in the yard. Inevitably, the ball hits the house, over and over again. With every thud, I expect a window to break. Finally, I can't stand it any more and lean out and shout for them to stop. Any possibility of doing work in the office is gone, and this makes me an ornery cuss.

I think back to the Wednesday before Easter break, to Little Michael's last after-school basketball league game. His middle school team was losing badly—the opposing team had one big lumbering ox of a kid, just past the onset of puberty, who used his size to intimidate the smaller boys. He didn't need to run across the court, which he couldn't do anyway. He'd just surround a smaller player with his bulk, glaring. He'd raise his thick, pasty arms to block out everything but the sight of his beady little eyes.

His opponents would cave in quickly. Slack-shouldered and frightened, they'd make their way to the bench feeling overpowered and diminished. The big beast fed on their despair, giving each an evil little grin before lumbering on to his next victim.

Watching the game, I'd grown more and more angry at his antics, frustrated that the coaches and referees did nothing to intercede. I wanted to wipe the supercilious little smirk off his fleshy face, and I wasn't the only one. Tracy, watching her son Richard get creamed every time he got the ball, was gritting her perfect teeth. Eyes flashing, she muttered, "I'm gonna get all New Jersey on that son of a bitch if he doesn't cut it out."

But he didn't, and she didn't, and neither did I. Always proper parents in public, we did our best to hold back. This was our kids' game, and we weren't about to wind up as a headline declaring "Pushy Parents Take Out Fat Guard." After the defeat, I hugged Michael and tried to encourage him, but he wasn't about to be consoled. "That fat kid wouldn't let us move. He just stood in our way like a wall, making faces and laughing at us. That's not playing basketball."

"Yeah, honey, I was surprised the coaches didn't do anything."

"They can't because he didn't break any rules. There's nothing that says you can't laugh when the other guy has the ball." He shook his head in disgust. "At least nobody on our team plays like that."

"That's because nobody on your team is that fat."

He snorted, feeling a little bit better.

I glance over at him now, sleeping in his seat down our row on the airplane. The three boys are lined up, window to aisle, their heads resting on the shoulders of the next. They look like little angels. I feel my cheeks redden, shamed—I'm no better than that lumbering bully, using my size and caustic nature to keep them in line.

Watching their gentle faces in sleep, I decide to take a new tack. Our trip to Hawaii will introduce a new "Gentle Dad," who only whispers admonishments wrapped in a warm blanket of praise and sweet words. The first time Matthew and Dereck start bickering in the back seat of the car on the way to the beach, I turn around and speak slowly and gently.

"Boys, it's not very nice of you to pick at each other like that, but I know your intention isn't to be mean. You are both such sweet loving boys, and when you do things that don't support your nature, it makes it hard on you. I know you really want to get along and enjoy each other's company. Why don't you try that?"

Dereck says, "Huh?"

Matthew says, "Is something wrong, Daddy John?"

"I don't want to yell at you anymore. I'm trying to learn to be gentle, to model for you how to behave in times of stress."

"Yuck. You don't sound like you."

"This is the new me. Learning to live with grace and ease."

When Michael leaves his wet, dirty towels and swimsuit on the hallway floor between our rooms, I take him aside and speak quietly again. "I know you didn't mean to leave these here, Michael, and I'm sure you just got distracted. You're always so responsible about picking things up and taking care of your belongings, I'm sure this was just an oversight. Would you consider picking them up and hanging them out in the yard, and then sweeping the sand off the floor?"

He stares out at me from under the mop of hair that nearly covers his eyes, "Who are you?"

"Your new, gentle dad."

"Ewww."

They take to giggling and doing their best to provoke me over the next couple of days. I can almost feel them nudge each other in the back of the car as we're driving, seeing what they can do to provoke me.

"Oww, stop it, Michael! Don't pinch me!"

"Dereck, quit farting."

"Matthew, stop putting your dirty feet in my face."

In the face of their collective farts, belches, pinching, and flying baseballs, I maintain my Zen-like calm. "My sons, you're all so wonderful and kind to each other. Wouldn't it be better just to make an effort to get along? When you make the effort, you'll be rewarded."

They roll their eyes and try again, but I refuse to rise to the bait. I'm having fun in this new persona. Even if the audience doesn't appreciate the method, they're at least showing signs it has some impact.

Finally, after a couple days of gentle parenting, they decide they've had enough. Together, they come to me to say, "We like the old Daddy John better. It's okay if you yell. You're supposed to yell. You don't even swear any more."

"But I'm setting a bad example for you when I yell. And you get all defeated and shut down, and then you won't talk. If I'm trying to correct your behavior, I can't get very far if you won't talk."

"We'll talk, we promise. It's too weird when you act like this. You're not being you."

"But I thought you don't like it when I yell."

"That's what dads do. And you're not as loud as J. K." J. K., the father of Matthew's best friend, coaches Matthew's softball team. He's an actor with a big, booming voice that could shatter brick. The seven year olds on his team shake when he yells, even though they know he's a big softy at heart.

"So I can go back to yelling?"

They nod and giggle. "And I can swear?" "You're going to, anyway."

I wrap my arms around all three of them and whisper into the air above their heads, "I love you boys more than I can say."

Then I draw back, staring into their eager faces. "Now go clean up your room. You don't want Aunt Suzanne to think you're pigs, do you?"

## Disappearing Act

The money sits on Daddy Michael's end of the desk, on a pile of receipts and candy wrappers and business cards that he likes to pull out of his pockets before dropping his pants on the floor. He likes his "stuff" to collect in an ever-widening pile on the end of the desk that is farthest from where I sit. It's his way to keep things organized, he says. It drives me nuts, but that's another story.

Dereck's eyes flicker over the cash when he comes into the room, his wish list of skateboard accessories in hand. "Daddy John, I want to order all of these things online," he says. "Can we do it?"

I glance down at the list; in typical Dereck fashion, it's complete and laid out in three columns, noting the item, description and cost. The total he wants to spend is $149.

"That's a lot of money, Dereck," I say. "I didn't know you had that much cash."

"I've been saving my allowance," he says.

"How much do you have?"

"Ninety-four dollars."

"Where were you going to get the rest, Dereck?"

"I dunno."

"Maybe you should prioritize this list, because you're not going to be able to afford all of it." This will be his third skateboard, so Daddy Michael and I have already decided whatever else he wants to buy, he'll have to either save for or earn.

He looks downcast. That's not what he wanted to hear. "Okay."

"What's the website?"

"Valsurf.com."

"It's the Web site for the skate shop in the Valley?"

"Yea."

"Honey, we'll just go there this afternoon after Matthew's softball game. That way you won't have to pay for shipping."

He smiles. "We can go?"

"Sure. But you're going to have to trim your list."

"Alright."

I head downstairs to make breakfast and get the boys moving. Daddy Michael's finished a long week of shooting, and he's got to run back and forth to the photo lab all afternoon. He'll make a stop there before the softball game and meet us. He comes down, in his usual predeparture rush, fussing and agitated. "Where did I leave my keys? Did you see the twenty dollars that was on my desk?"

"The keys are on the shelf above the desk, and I saw your money on the pile."

"It's not there now, and I looked all over it."

"It was there ten minutes ago."

"I know."

A little blond head perched over his bowl of cereal moves imperceptibly.

Daddy Michael looks at me, and suddenly I get it. The recognition makes me stop dead in my tracks. I open my mouth to starting yelling, but something stops me. A profound stillness takes hold, saying, *Wait. This is serious. Let this play out before you do anything.*

Looking over their heads at Michael, I have no clue how to handle this. He looks at me, and I know he feels the same. "We'll figure it out when I get back," he says, and kisses each of their heads.

We get to the game early, and while Matthew and his team are warming up, I ask Dereck to walk across the park with me to the bank. "Dereck, do you have any idea what happened to Daddy Michael's money?"

"No." He had been absolutely silent on the drive to the park, and now he won't look at me.

"Well, I can't help but wonder if you know something about it. You and I were the only ones in the office before it disappeared, and I know you saw it there. And I know you wanted to buy more things than you had money for."

"I didn't take it."

"I'm not saying you did, Dereck. I'm just saying it looks suspicious."

"I didn't take it." But he still won't look at me.

"I'm not saying you took it. I know you know better. I know you believe stealing is wrong."

He finally looks at me, clutching his stomach. "What's wrong, Dereck?"

"My stomach hurts."

"I'm sorry. Do we need to go back and sit down?"

He shakes his head no, and we continue walking. "You know, when you showed me the things you wanted to buy today, and you said you didn't have enough money, I thought you might ask me if we'd pay for it, or if there was some way you could earn the difference."

"You did?"

"Of course. Have we ever said no when you've asked for something? Or didn't try to help you figure out a way to earn it?"

"No."

"Sometimes when people steal something, they're afraid to believe that God or their parents are going to take care of them. So they do something they shouldn't, and then they realize it was a mistake not to trust. Does that make sense?

"Yeah." He's starting to bend over now, clutching his stomach even tighter.

"Well, honey, if there's something you want to tell me, I'm here."

He shakes his head no, and I let him wallow in his misery. All through the game, he sits hunched over on the bleachers, barely paying attention. On the way home, I ask his brothers, "Hey, did either of you see Daddy Michael's money?" Of course, they say no, but from the way Little Michael looks at Dereck, he's already figured out what's going on.

When we get home, Dereck doesn't ask if we can go to the skate shop, but takes to his bed, falling asleep immediately. Four hours later, he comes into the kitchen, still clutching his stomach and hunched over.

"How are you feeling, Dereck?"

"Okay."

"Got something to tell me?"

He looks up and whispers, "Not here."

I nod, and he follows me up to our office. He's carrying his wallet, and when he closes the door, he opens it and takes out a twenty-dollar bill. "I took Daddy Michael's money."

"Thank you for admitting it. Why did you steal it, honey?"

"I wanted all the stuff for my skateboard."

"Did you think we wouldn't figure it out?"

"I dunno."

"Do you think you felt sick this afternoon because you realized stealing was wrong?"

"Yes." He hangs his head.

"I'm glad for that. I'm really disappointed in you, Dereck. I know you know better."

He shakes his head; he is even more disappointed in himself. But at least now that he's made his confession, he's able to sit up straight.

"What do you think your consequence should be for stealing, Dereck?"

"I dunno."

"I'm not sure either. Daddy Michael and I are going to have to discuss it, and we'll all sit down together and talk about it. When he gets home, you need to tell him what you've done."

"I know."

"Come over here." He gets up from his chair and climbs into my lap, wrapping his arms around my neck. "Dereck, just so you know, I'm disappointed by what you did, But that doesn't mean I don't love you. No matter what you do, Daddy Michael and I are always going to love you—and always try to help you do what is right."

After he leaves, I find myself wrapped in the stillness that had first come over me when we realized what he'd done. There could be myriad reasons why he decided to steal, but instinctively I knew what was at its core. Some children steal for kicks, some because it is the only way they know to get what they want.

But Dereck was different: he was undergoing an almost spiritual transformation, getting rid of the old and taking on the new. Long before he came to us, he'd been taught that deceit and deception were the only way to survive in a deeply unfriendly world. It was a lesson that may have served him well when he and his brothers had to fend for themselves, but it was one he no longer needed.

That afternoon, at the tender age of eleven, Dereck had waged an epic battle in his own heart, and even if he'd made the wrong choice to begin with, he'd finally come to a place where he choose to act on what he knew was right.

No consequence we could give him would ever teach him that lesson as fully.

When Michael called and I told him Dereck had finally confessed, he sounded exasperated. "How do we get him to understand he just doesn't need to do stuff like that anymore?"

"I think he's begun to figure that out," I replied. "But I was starting to worry we'd have to lock up all the cash around the house."

"I could never do that. And besides, I don't think he'll pull a stunt like this again. He's learned his lesson. But you know, I think that's the hardest part. I never thought it would be so difficult to let them learn their lessons the hard way."

"Me either. It was all I could do not to pull that confession out of his mouth. But that wouldn't have done any good. He had to get to the place where he could do it on his own."

"Boy, aren't you glad he did?"

"Yeah."

"I'll be home soon, and we can figure out what his consequence should be."

As we hung up, a verse from the Book of Proverbs popped into my head: "Train up a child in the way he should go, and when he is old, he will not depart from it."

I sat mulling those words over, and the weight of our responsibility suddenly felt unbearably heavy. After a day like today, I had no clue if we were doing the right thing or not. This wasn't simple, like showing him how to brush his teeth or how to do long division. This was about how to make right choices in life. How could be sure we were doing it right?

I sat with that feeling a while longer, my head in my hands. Slowly, I realized training was all about showing him what we do ourselves. He'd learn from us, just as he'd learned from his mother. And ultimately, the responsibility was his—he would choose what to follow. Much as we might want to, we couldn't make those decisions for him. All we could do is love him and try to guide his way.

## Naked

Until a few weeks ago, seven-year-old Matthew thought nothing of flying around the house naked after his shower, dripping water and exulting in the freedom of wearing no clothes.

But something changed.

Suddenly, he'd cover himself if we walked in while he was getting dressed for school, giggling and looking sheepish. "What's up, Matthew?" I'd ask.

"I'm naked," he'd shout, pivoting away, all the while keeping his eyes on me to see how I'd react.

I don't have a lot of patience in the morning. "Hurry up, Matthew! We've got to leave for school in five minutes and you haven't eaten breakfast. It's not like we haven't seen you naked before. Get moving!"

He'd fall to the floor to pull on his underwear, almost deflated I wasn't making a big deal of his natural state.

*What is going on with him?* I wondered. *He must be going through some new phase that has made him newly conscious of his body. He's got a long way to go before he hits puberty. Maybe he feels grown-up because his front teeth are finally coming in.*

Then JK called after Matthew had a sleepover with his son Joe. "I thought you might want to know about something that happened last night," he said. "Joe told me he and Matthew got into a pinching game and then they started smacking and pulling at each other's private parts. Joe got uncomfortable and asked Matthew to stop. But Matthew was pretty wound up and didn't. It's kid stuff, and I don't think it's a big deal. But I'd want to know if my kid was doing that at someone else's house."

*Oh, Jesus*, I thought, and I thanked JK for giving us the head's up. "We'll talk to Matthew, and I suspect he's going to be apologizing to Joe soon."

"No big deal," JK said again.

*But you wouldn't call unless it was*, I said to myself, and I thanked him again before saying good-bye.

When I hung up, I didn't know whether to laugh or cry. Sex games at seven. Matthew had complained earlier about "show and tell" in the school bathroom, but the pinching and pulling was new. Welcome to the next phase in his psychosexual development.

137

When I hit an issue I don't know how to handle, I call my mom. And, as usual, her advice was succinct and to the point. "Put a stop to it right now. He's too young to be doing stuff like that. If you don't teach him now, none of the kids are going to want to play with him."

When I tell Michael what my mom said, he shakes his head; he's the real softie in this household. "I don't know how we stop him. We don't want to teach Matthew that exploring his body is something to be ashamed of, so if we come down too hard, it's going to send the wrong message."

"But we do need to teach him what's appropriate and what's not. I wouldn't be so concerned if he'd stopped when Joe asked him to."

When I ask Matthew if something happened with Joe, he looks at me blankly.

I try again. "Did Joe get upset about something while you were playing a game?"

Again, the blank stare.

"No?" I continued. "Did you play a pinching game?"

He looks puzzled for a moment and starts to get teary-eyed. He knows he's about to get into trouble, but he can't figure out why. "Yes."

"What happened, Matthew?"

"Nothing," he wails, and his little checks turn bright red. "What did I do?"

"Matthew, did you pinch and pull at Joe's privates after he asked you not to?"

Suddenly, he gets it, and the real wailing starts. I can't tell if he's more embarrassed than upset, but he quickly works himself into such a lather he's hiccupping and gasping for air. His brothers come running into the room, worried, and even after I signal they should leave, they hover around the door until I shut it firmly and tell them to go away.

I let him go for a few moments, and the wailing gradually turns into a sputter. "Matthew, I need to know if that's what happened."

"Yes."

"Why didn't you stop when Joe asked you to?"

"I don't know."

"I want you to know I'm not upset because you were playing the game. I'm upset because you didn't stop when Joe asked you to."

The wailing stops completely. "Huh?"

"Matthew, it's normal to play games like that when you're seven. It's normal to be curious about what other people look like. But when someone tells you they are uncomfortable, you've got to stop immediately. Remember how you told me you didn't like it when Jason and Eduardo were playing games in the bathroom at school?"

He nods.

"You told them you didn't like it, and they stopped doing it in front of you, didn't they?"

He nods again.

"That's because they were showing respect for you. When you're doing something someone else doesn't like, you have to do the same thing."

He's wide-eyed. "Oh."

"Were you showing Joe respect when you wouldn't stop?"

"No."

"How do you think that made Joe feel?"

"Not very good."

"So what do you think you need to do?"

"Tell Joe I'm sorry."

"Yep. And don't you think you should apologize to JK, too?"

He looks sheepish. "But it's embarrassing." He's learned that word from Dereck.

"All the more reason to apologize."

He knows he can't get out of it, so he agrees.

Again, I feel like I'm navigating a tightrope. We don't have a problem showing our kids how to use their feet and hands and ears. But get the penis involved, and we get a little nervous. How do we teach Matthew not to be ashamed about his curiosity but learn to respect other's bodies and boundaries?

There's no question little boys are fascinated with their penises, and that fascination can carry over into adulthood. I once went out with someone who had a nickname for his, and he'd talk about it like it was a third person. "Jackson likes this, and Jackson likes that," he'd say, evidently proud it had a mind of its own.

Jackson's handler and I soon parted ways; it was a bit too weird for me. But I realize every man I know who's not afraid to admit it carries some secret peccadillo about his penis. It's too small or too big or too thin or too thick, or it goes in a direction he doesn't like. It may be lighter or darker than the rest of his body, or too hairy or not hairy enough. The depth and intensity of our penile introspection is endless.

We'd be loath to admit it, but most men fret about our penises in the same way a lot of women fret about their breasts or hips or tummies. Somewhere along the way, shame overcomes the delight we are born with, and we carry that dissatisfaction for the rest of our lives. We forget we're created in the image of God, spontaneous erections and all.

It's all about socialization, I think. Michael and Dereck came to us already conditioned to feel shame. When they get up each morning, they run to the bathroom hunched over, hands covering their genitals, petrified something's going to pop out and scare everybody.

Matthew's not quite there yet. Maybe we can help him realize all the funny things his body might do are normal. Maybe we can encourage him to hang on to his sense of play and his childlike curiosity. Maybe we can help him realize that the things we find embarrassing about ourselves are often the things we're not supposed to take too seriously.

And maybe, just maybe, we can learn along with Matthew that the only truly shameful thing about being a boy is to let ourselves become disconnected from our bodies.

## Sending Pictures

I was feeling guilty, and I wasn't sure why. Michael's eighth grade graduation pictures were in their envelope, and we hadn't started sending them out yet. I kept looking at them, wondering if we should send a picture to his birth mom.

I asked him, and he shrugged. "Why? She won't do anything with it."

The pictures sat on my desk, and even though the post office box we'd rented in case she wanted to write us remained empty, something gnawed at me until I decided to act.

It only took a few minutes to knock out a simple, almost breezy, letter, just four paragraphs filled with their summer plans and activities. I pulled out Michael's picture, so serious in his cap and gown, along with smiling ones of Dereck and Matthew, put them in an envelope along with the letter, and dropped it in the mailbox.

I had no idea what condition she would be in when she received it, nor how she would react. I just knew she loved her kids as best she was able, and that any mother would probably want to see pictures of children she hadn't seen in two years.

"Don't you wonder if she'll feel like you're rubbing it in?" my friend Les asked while we were catching up over lunch.

"I don't know. On one hand, I feel so sorry for her. But then I want to make sure she really gets the fact her kids are doing better now than when they were taken away from her. It's snarky, but it's true."

"That's pretty normal, though, isn't it?"

"Sure. But we have to be on guard all the time. It makes not one bit of difference what we think of the boys' mom. If we ever said anything negative about her, it would come back to haunt us."

A couple days later, we're in the office filling out the paperwork for the boys' summer camps. They have to show their immunization records, so we pull out the old forms that have their birth names on them.

Michael picks up his form and looks at his old name, a bit confused. "Isn't our name changed?"

"Yes, that's the old immunization record we got when you came to us."

"But that's not our name anymore, right?"

"Right. Your name was legally changed when you were adopted."

He nods, still confused. "But what about old stuff?"

"Remember when we got your new birth certificates?" He nods. "When we adopted you, your birth certificate was changed, and Daddy Michael and I are listed as your parents. The old birth certificates were destroyed, so from now on, any official record will list us as your parents."

He looks relieved. "Good." He gets up from the floor and kisses the top of my head.

After the boys go back downstairs, I look at Big Michael. "What was that all about?"

"Beats me. If he wants us to know, he'll figure out a way to tell us."

I would love to believe Little Michael's reaction is all about being entranced by living with us, but I know the truth lies elsewhere. He definitely gets frustrated by my nagging about picking up his clothes and helping around the house, and he hates it when Daddy Michael makes him do work in the yard.

The minute he thinks he's going to be tapped for a chore, he starts rubbing his head and eyes like he has poison ivy. "I have a headache," he says, as if we were taken in the first twenty times he tried it as an excuse.

"Take some Tylenol and start vacuuming," I'll order.

"Awww, do I have to?" is the standard reply. But he does it, somewhat grudgingly and with the least amount of effort he can possibly muster. He's a typical teenager, and of course, it is maddening.

He's at that age where he not-so-subtly challenges me on my own stuff. "Michael, don't you think you could manage to polish the entire dining room table instead of just parts of it?"

"Just because you think it has to be perfect doesn't mean I think it has to be perfect."

In his slightly twisted teenage logic, of course he's right. The first time he tried it, the hair bristled on the back of my neck, and I felt my chest puffing out instinctively. *Who the hell does he think he is, calling me on my shit?*

It's my mother's voice rattling around in my head, and of course, it stops me in my tracks. The last time she tried to hit me, I was about Michael's age and in the middle of some smart-ass comment to goad her. Instead of running away, I turned around and looked down at her. She suddenly realized I was a head taller and stopped dead in her tracks. She started giggling, and I laughed with her, and it never happened again. I wish I could say I never gave her cause again to want to smack me, but of course, that isn't true.

Michael's forging his own identity, and he's right to do it. What does it really matter that he can still write his name in the dust on a third of the table? For the first time in his life, he's learning to stick up for himself, and even if he's gawky and a little inappropriate in the way he does it, he's got to have the space to try.

His graduation is in two weeks, and I get an e-mail from Stephen, the headmaster of Michael's school, saying Michael's been selected to introduce the keynote speaker, Los Angeles City Council President Eric Garcetti. He's got to rehearse his introduction, and Stephen wants me to work with Michael to help him prepare.

Of course, I gush when we pick him up from school that night. "Michael, do you realize what a big honor this is? We are so proud of you."

He just rolls his eyes. "I have to say a lot of stuff."

"We'll work on it this weekend, so you can get more comfortable with the words."

"Awww, do I have to?"

On Saturday evening, we go to our friend Richard's to swim; it's been a blazingly hot day, and the boys scream and splash and drag the dogs into the pool. After, Michael wraps himself in a towel and plops in my lap, leaning against me.

"Hey, you're getting me all wet."

He shakes his big clump of wet hair in response. Leaning back even more, he whispers, "Daddy John?"

"Yes, honey?"

"The speech is hard. I don't think I can do it."

"We can work on it tonight. I know you can do it."

"I don't wanna."

"Michael, Mr. Stephen picked you specifically out of all your class because he knew you could. He has faith in you."

He shakes his head again, and I whisper, "Michael, this is one of the few times you'll ever hear me say something is nonnegotiable. I know you can do it, and Mr. Stephen knows you can do it. You just have to believe you can."

Later he sits at the kitchen counter and reads his introduction out loud. He's right. It is hard; it was probably written by someone on Garcetti's staff who has no clue an eighth grader is going to read it.

He reads and I stop him, correcting pronunciation and trying to help him catch a rhythm. He can't for the life of him pronounce "Gorbachev," and he stumbles on it, over and over. His frustration is enormous, and he finally slams the paper on the counter. "I can't do it."

"Yes, you can, honey. Here. Let's think about this like a song. Some words need a whole note, and some a quarter note. And there's a rest in between sentences. Let's mark it up like it was a song, and see how it sounds."

He suddenly gets it, and we work through the text, talking about phrasing and what to emphasize and where to pause. His tenth reading is infinitely better. "That's great, Michael. You've got it just right. Let's stop here and let your mind absorb it, and I'll listen to you again tomorrow."

He hugs me and says, "Thanks, Daddy John."

What a wide fence he's trying to straddle, our son, living in this awkward space between being a boy and a man. Crawling into my lap one minute, squaring his shoulders to challenge me the next, he's a teenaged shape-shifter, leaping from baby to adult in a flash of hormone-charged energy.

I know it's as confusing to him as it is to us. He's trying on a new persona without really being sure he wants to give up the old. But no matter who he winds up being at any given moment, all he really wants is consistent understanding and love. Our constancy can make his own wobbliness that much easier to handle.

I'm still not sure it was okay for me to send his mother his graduation picture. He wants to believe that if he shuts her and her memory out, the hurt will go away. Of course I know better. With so much of his life in flux, he isn't ready or able to take it on, and we could never force him. But we can keep the channel open while he cannot, so that when he does decide it is time, it will be easier for him to reconnect and heal—when he's ready, and on his own terms.

## Lean on Me

Michael's eighth grade graduation party is a major event, held in a big house in a gated community that had been carved out of the property that was once Cecil B. DeMille's estate. Three moms with a lot of time planned the party within an inch of its life, building in surprises galore for the kids, their friends, and their fellow parents.

I don't like surprises.

While the kids are swooshing down the sixty-foot tiled slide into the pool, the parents are summoned into the hosts' recording studio/media room. "We're going to sing to the kids," one of the chirpy planning moms announces, handing out the sheet music. From behind her steps the school's music director and two guitarists; before we have time to react, we are rehearsing.

I don't like to sing in public.

The rest of the parents dive in, good-natured and laughing, Daddy Michael included. He loves this kind of stuff. I feel like a real stick-in-the mud, horrified that I have to perform in public. I can't make myself master the harmony line or the muddled choreography we are all expected to learn in five minutes. As much as I like all the parents and the kids, this is not how I want to hang out at a party.

I try to be a good sport.

Through gritted teeth, I join the parents up front after the boys have each gotten special awards. The guitar starts, the music director cues us. I take a deep breath and open my mouth. But nothing comes out. Then I look at Little Michael, sitting in the first row, a big grin on his face. And I remember how we'd had to coax him into performing with his classmates in the school musical, and how the first time he was up on stage, he was so shy he couldn't lift his head. He'd forced himself to perform. Now he is absolutely delighted his dads are going to sing.

I decide to sing for him.

I try again, but no sound comes out. Instead, I find my eyes getting wet. The chirpy moms have picked their song well; the words hit me hard:

> *Lean on me*
> *when you're not strong,*
> *and I'll be your friend.*
> *I'll help to carry you.*

Little Michael sees my wet eyes, sees me struggling, and knows immediately what is going on. He locks his eyes on mine, and he nods his encouragement, just like we did with him his first time on stage. I nod back, fortified.

I open my mouth again and sing my guts out.

"Good job, Daddy John," he says, punching my arm when it is over. Then he turns and dives into the pool, squealing and splashing with his friends.

# Part III

## Joy Comes in the Morning

It is not how much you do, but how much love you put in the doing.
—*Mother Teresa*

Our third year as a family proved a crucible, a year that changed us—changed me—forever.

Tennyson wrote in *In Memoriam: 27*, "Tis better to have loved and lost than never to have loved at all." He may have been right. But loss brings with it the inevitable question, "Can I continue to love, even if it means opening myself to potential pain again?"

This is, I believe, the truest test of our humanness, to lose and continue to love. And if we emerge from that dark night, we find we have been deepened, richer, burnished like copper over a hot flame.

## New Roommates

We're having a dinner party, the adults gathered around the dining room table and the kids at the kitchen counter just a few feet away. Anthony glances around to see if the boys are listening, and then whispers conspiratorially across the dinner table, "They started doing cocaine in the Jacuzzi just before I left the house."

"They did what?" I practically shout before I can help myself. All three boys, sitting nearby at the kitchen counter, turn and stare at me. They know they're going to hear something juicy.

Anthony looks at them and at the adults around the dinner table, and he says, "We'll have to finish this discussion later."

"Damn right we will." I glare at him, and he gives me a small, self-satisfied smile. We have a kind of friendship that is like brothers—competitive and loving and irritating, all at the same time. He knows exactly how to get under my skin, what buttons to push to get a rise out of me.

He had invited two buddies to rent the upstairs of his house, complaining he felt lonely and that his house was too big to live in alone. Great intention, but the pair shared his affinity for crystal meth and coke; they have a long history of partying together. While Anthony has made an effort to get clean, it was evident they had not; this is trouble, no doubt about it.

They'd just moved in this afternoon. "I see they didn't waste any time," I mutter.

Glancing at our friends around the table, I can tell I'm not the only one who's deeply concerned. None of us wants to go through one of Anthony's binges again. He'll suddenly disappear for a week or more, not answering his door or returning phone calls. He only reaches out when he senses things have gotten out of control.

We've all been through the paranoid hallucinations, him sleeping with a baseball bat on his living room couch, him being walked home by concerned neighbors who find him wandering the neighborhood at 3 AM. We've watched nasty, opportunistic illnesses beat down his immune system, sat with him through months of illness and recovery. Every binge makes him physically weaker. Having this temptation right under his nose could destroy him.

And the horrible thing is, we all know he wants it that way.

148

As soon as the boys finish and go upstairs to watch a movie, I turn to Anthony. "What the hell is going on?"

His grin is as broad as a crocodile's. "What do you mean?" He's clearly enjoying the situation, loving being the center of attention.

"They start doing coke before they have a chance to unpack?"

"They wanted to celebrate. It's no big deal."

"They bring illegal substances into your house and do it in front of you. And that's not a big deal?"

"No. Should it be?"

Our friend Richard interjects. "Come on, Anthony. You know better. You don't need that stuff in your house."

"I don't know why you're all so concerned. Let's change the subject." Anthony looks around the table, satisfied. He's created the drama he was looking for. He's put us all on notice that he's going to toy with temptation, and he's made it clear we can't do anything to stop him.

I can't contain myself. "Anthony, what kind of monsters snort coke right in front you on the first day they move in? Get rid of them. Or if you're afraid to, I'll be happy to have that conversation for you." I glare at him. "Do you want me to take care of this?"

Michael, at the other end of the table, looks at me and shakes his head. He knows it will do no good.

But I sail on, ready to deliver what I hope will be the *coup de grace*. "One last thing, then, Anthony. Our boys will never step foot in your house while they're living there. I don't want them seeing that stuff, even if you choose to turn a blind eye."

His eyes cloud for just a moment, and I think I may have finally gotten through to him. But he straightens up and says quietly, "I don't think you're being fair, but I can't stop you."

I finally stop, realizing I may have gone too far. We perch on the edge of the precipice, too afraid to look down, but too afraid to back away. Our dinner ends in awkward silence.

Like so many addicts, Anthony is a walking contradiction. When he's honest, he can acknowledge his self-destructive behavior. But he loves to live in a world of cat-and-mouse games, pushing his friends to give the value to his life that he refuses to give it himself.

And like so many people who love addicts, I play right along with him, speaking my truth but not holding him accountable, afraid that if I do, he'll slip farther down the path of self-destruction.

The following Friday, Michael and I get a rare dinner out without the boys. As we're leaving the restaurant, full and feeling the margaritas, we walk by Brian, one of the cokeheads inhabiting Anthony's upper room. Michael, more gracious than I, says hello. I glower as I push by, refusing to meet his expectant, slightly watery eyes.

The phone rings early the next morning. When I answer, Anthony says, "Brian thought you were rude not to say hello last night."

"He's lucky I didn't punch him in the face."

"What's Brian done to you? He couldn't understand why you wouldn't say hello."

"Would you like me to tell him, Anthony?"

He says gently, "It would make things easier for me if you made an effort to be nice."

I pause, caught short. Suddenly, the freight-train diatribe that has been my only conversation with Anthony for weeks runs off-track. "You've made so much progress over the past year, Anthony. I'm so proud of you. Their moving in makes me really afraid for you."

"Don't let your fear make you so angry. I understand how much you worry about me. I don't want to get myself in trouble again. I actually went to my dealer and asked him to not sell to me, no matter how much I beg."

"Anthony …" I start to say something, but I'm not sure what. How do you respond to a confession like that? "Alright. I'll try."

"Thank you."

And there it is. Perhaps a small breakthrough, or perhaps it is just wily Anthony, challenging me in an effort to deflect attention from himself. Either way, he's right about one thing. I'm afraid, and I've let that fear take shape as white-hot rage. I rail at Anthony, at Brian, at the whole situation, because I am afraid one more binge will kill him. So I try to control Anthony's behavior, attempting to shame and cajole and bully him into bending to my will.

But I have no control—not over his cocky confidence, so sure he can toy with exposure; not over the lure of getting high; not over the inevitable toll using will take on his health and spirit.

This is Anthony's demon, Anthony's life, Anthony's choice.

And my choice is how I respond. The moment he told me he was inviting Brian and Bobby to move in, it was like flipping a switch. It opened the current of anger that surged through me like a life force, giving it one more place to surface.

My anger has nothing to do with Anthony and everything to do with me. And if I really love Anthony, if I really care about the situation he is in, I have to separate them. I have to sit with my anger, play with it, stroke it instead of stoke it, try to understand. And as I do, understanding slowly peels away layer upon layer.

I've lost too many friends in my life, and I don't want to lose one more. I'm angry that Anthony, who has nearly died more than once, has been given the gift of extra time and chooses to throw it away. I'm angry because the seeds of Anthony's self-destruction run deep in the soil of his family's disapproval. I'm angry because he wants love so desperately he's willing to kill himself to get it.

I want to cry for Anthony—and for the desperate fear that sits in the pit of my stomach. But I won't. To cry would feel like giving in, and I won't give in to this fear. Not for Anthony, and not for me. I need to keep up the fight, to give him the courage he might not have himself, and I hope against hope he won't give in.

## Mishap on the Train

Matthew walks from his seat on the train to mine, two rows up. "Daddy John, my pee-pee is stuck on my bathing suit."

Everyone within hearing distance turns and stares.

"It's stuck?"

"Yes. I can't get it out. And I have to go to the bathroom."

"Okay. I'll go to the bathroom with you and see what I can do."

We're on a packed train from Los Angeles to San Diego, Matthew and I. We're on our way to meet Daddy Michael and Dereck, who had gone down the day before. We'll stay in San Diego overnight and pick up Little Michael on his last day of band camp.

We'd scrambled to get to the train. Matthew was late getting back from his day camp field trip to the beach, and we'd run to the train at the last minute, lucky to get the last three seats in the car. Matthew was still wearing his bathing suit and flip-flops.

In the tiny bathroom, Matthew starts to pull down his suit, but stops halfway, wincing. Through one of the minute holes of the suit's mesh inner lining, a swollen piece of foreskin sticks out, all red and purple and blue.

The trapped skin had swollen to four times its normal size.

Looking at it, my stomach turns over. "Oh, Matthew. How did this happen?"

"I don't know. I think it happened in the water."

"You didn't ask one of the counselors for help?"

"No. I thought they would get mad."

He tries to shake it free, but there's at least a quarter inch of swollen skin. It won't budge. "It hurts, Daddy John. I'm afraid to pee."

I have no idea what to do. "We'll figure something out, Matthew."

Matthew's face turns red, and he starts to cry. "You're not going to cut it off?"

"Oh, no, honey. Maybe we can use some soap to lubricate it, and then we can get it to slide out. Do you want to try that?"

He looks scared, but nods his head. We got the soap and tried to cover all the skin that was exposed.

"Okay, Matthew. We'll try to slide it out. Are you ready?"

He nods again, and slowly, I begin to work the skin free.

It isn't easy, but it begins to give way, and with a little pop, it comes out. The place where it had been lodged against the mesh is scraped; it starts to bleed immediately.

Seeing the blood, Matthew's face turned white. "It got cut off! It got cut off!" He shakes uncontrollably.

I grab him and hug him. "It's okay, Matthew. Your skin got scraped where it was stuck. Nothing got cut off. It's just like scraping your finger."

Just then, the train lurches to a stop; we're in San Diego. I try to clean him off and clean up the blood on the floor of the bathroom.

"Honey, we're here. Can we get your underwear and shorts on? We'll get some Neosporin when we get off the train, and that will help it feel better."

Still shaking, tears streaming down his cheeks, we get him dressed. He's so upset, he refuses to walk. I have to carry him down the train aisle, past all the departing passengers.

We manage to get off the train and down the track to where Michael and Dereck are waiting. When he sees them, Matthew turns his face into my neck, and his tears run down onto my shirt. He's embarrassed.

As we walk to the hotel, I try to explain what happened to Michael. Outside, I'm as calm as Matthew is upset. But inside, I'm a wreck. I have a vision of Matthew at age forty, sitting with a therapist, analyzing his fears of castration.

But Matthew's a trooper, and as he calms down, he decides he's ready to walk. After a couple of tentative steps, he moves like nothing ever happened.

He does a couple of kung fu kicks on the sidewalk, and turns to Dereck to tell him what happened. When Dereck grimaces and says, "Ewwwww ..." Matthew's delighted.

This is a story he's going to tell over and over.

Seeing him laugh, I finally relax. There won't be any lasting scars—on his poor little uncircumcised penis, or in his head.

We're just about at the hotel when he turns to me. "Daddy John?"

"Yes, honey?"

"Thank you for pulling it out. I thought I'd have to wear my bathing suit forever."

*John Sonego*

"That's okay, Matthew. I'm glad we got it out, too."

## Dereck Goes to Camp

When I answer the phone, all I hear are sniffles and a weak little "gurrumph ..."

It's Dereck, away at football camp, calling for the tenth time today. He's making that traditional right of passage—the first time away from home on his own—and he's not liking it one bit.

"Hi, honey. How was football practice this afternoon?"

I hear a long, soulful sigh, followed by a warbled, "I wanna come home. Will you come and pick me up?"

"Dereck, every time we talk, you say you want to come home, and then you decide you want to stay. Did you have a good time playing football today?"

"Yes."

"Are you having fun with your roommate?"

"Yes."

"Don't you want to play in the exhibition game on Thursday? That's only a day away."

"Yes."

"There's only one more day of practice. Do you think you can do that?"

Another long sigh. "Yes ... but you are coming to my game, aren't you? It's at nine o'clock."

"Yes, Dereck, we'll be there on Thursday morning."

"Okay. I just wanted to be sure." Another sniffle, and I can hear his roommate Jason calling him to go to dinner.

"Dereck, you shouldn't make Jason wait. Why don't you call again tonight before you go to bed? We can pray together over the phone."

"Okay. Daddy John?"

"Yes?"

"I love you."

"I love you, too. And I'm proud of you for deciding to stick it out."

Dereck doesn't know it, but we expected he would have a hard time. He'd picked the camp, even though it had a grueling practice schedule of eight or nine hours on the field each day. We'd tried to suggest alternatives, but his mind was made up. It was this football camp or nothing.

So Michael drove him down on Sunday afternoon and, without telling Dereck, stayed in a hotel nearby, just so he could check on him the next day.

Standing in a parking garage adjacent to the field, he watched through binoculars for hours, calling me with reports.

"Yep. He's stomping off the field! He's pissed because he missed the pass. He looks okay, though. Jeez, he's got the whitest legs of any kid here."

It's heartbreaking to hear your kid cry, heartbreaking to talk him out of coming home, heartbreaking to watch him struggle from a distance. Given our druthers, we'd want nothing more than to scoop him up and bring him home.

But one of the greatest gifts we can give our children is the gift of letting go.

This is an important step for Dereck, an eleven-year-old assertion of independence. He loves football, and he wants to play in high school and college. He'd made the smart choice, finding the camp that has turned out scores of champions, knowing he would learn to play better.

Each time he calls, we remind him we love him, we are always with him wherever he is, and that there's a great big Dereck-sized hole at home that only he can fill.

We know the day will come when he won't be around to fill that hole; adulthood is not that far away. So we savor this moment, thankful he's still enough of a kid to be homesick, still enough of a kid to declare he misses us, still enough of a kid that our support means the world.

By Wednesday night, when he called to say good night and to remind us again about the starting time for his game in the morning, there was a note of triumph in his voice. He'd gotten this far, and tomorrow, after the Offense-Defense Football Camp Super Bowl, he would come home.

## His Perfect Life

I don't remember taking notes when the phone call came, but I found them days later, scrawled on a scrap of paper.

> *He was in good spirits.*
> *The maid thought he was asleep so she didn't disturb him.*
> *They found him with a plastic bag over his head.*

Nothing prepares you for a phone call like this, the discombobulated voice that suddenly sounds a million miles away. Writing by rote somehow served to create distance from the truth, the absolute sorrow I couldn't yet absorb.

To choose to end your life is a decision you can't imagine anyone ever making. And so it was with our friend, Anthony.

Michael and I were both sitting in the office when the call came. And as the word spread, our phone kept ringing and ringing and ringing, friend after friend calling, all in shock, all filled with questions.

We knew he was worn out. We knew he'd struggled with disease and addiction for years. We knew he'd been seeing a psychiatrist who'd prescribed antidepressants that didn't seem to work. Slowly, we pieced together that he'd been whispering to each of us, singly and without drama, that he felt he no longer had a purpose.

But each of us had enjoyed time with him in the last few days of his life, when he was merry and focused and completely engaged in conversation and activity. How could he operate in such a dichotomy, enjoying life so thoroughly while planning its end?

This is the mystery I cannot understand.

When his body was released from the coroner, his family invited me to go with them to view it before cremation. I went, wondering if it would give me some clue. It could be a chance to say good-bye, to have one last look, to whisper the questions only he could answer.

Once the door was opened and we stepped into the tiny room, I knew I would have no answers. The body that lay there, covered by a sheet, was not the friend I knew. Eyes closed, the skin discolored and already decomposing, lips tightly shut in a way they'd never been in life; the only thing that reminded me of the living Anthony was his hair, which had grown out even more since I'd seen him last.

He'd wanted me to cut it the last night we'd spent together, when he came to the house for dinner and to go to the Hollywood Bowl. But there hadn't been enough time, and I'd promised to cut it early the next week.

By then, it was too late.

Our conversation that night: haircuts and fried chicken, the overgrown roses on the deck, the long drive he hated to make alone on his way to his family's annual camping trip. He worried his mom wouldn't like to use the communal bathroom in the campground. Could he buy the kids ice cream during intermission? Conversation in quick bits and starts, with kids interrupting and glasses to be refilled and plates to be cleared and sweatshirts to gather. And a quick whispered aside, as he sat on my left at the place he always took at our table, telling me he didn't want to be around any longer.

It went right over my head.

Later, I realized Anthony had planned this last event with us carefully. Our first experience of him as a family, the night the boys moved in, was a concert at the Hollywood Bowl. Of course he would make sure the last experience we had with him as a family would be the same.

The coroner's report won't be released for at least thirty days, and while his family still wants to hear the specifics of how he died, it doesn't matter to me. It is done, and the details no longer matter.

But the night after his funeral, when all the frantic preparation was over and we were all left with that dull reality he was no longer there, I dreamt of him. In my dream, I could only see his thick, strong hands, working on the butcher block counter in his kitchen, calmly mixing pills and turning it all into a liquid potion.

Anthony the master chemist, Anthony the anesthesiologist, whose mind was a walking pharmacist's reference, knew exactly what he was doing. The liquid would be easier to absorb, and he would be less likely to vomit it up.

I woke, shaking, babbling a prayer to take this dream away—I didn't want to know, didn't need to know, let me sleep again, I asked, and have some pleasant dream that will wipe this away.

I fell asleep and dreamt the same dream.

Somehow, I believe he wanted me to know.

I wonder now if Anthony's ability to plan his death while enjoying his life is simply a more advanced approach to the human experience.

From the moment each of us is born, we move unalterably to our deaths, and throughout our lives we experience a continual process of little deaths that enable life to continue until our end.

Scientists know something of this from their study of how our bodies work. Every day, certain cells throughout our bodies automatically relinquish their lives in a process called apoptosis. It is an orderly process scientists have learned is necessary for our ongoing survival. In fact, if a cell forgets to die, it leads to the development of cancerous tumors that feed on the body that gives the cell life.

A highly functioning cell *knows* when its work is done and it is time to move on.

Within the tight constraints of his own sense of order, Anthony had done everything he could do. His stunted medical career, cut short by disease, had been brilliant, but was long over. He had devoted himself to volunteer work to the point of exhaustion; he left his imprint on his city and on the volunteers he served with, people who grew to lean on and love him.

And he left an indelible mark on the next generation, his nieces and nephews, both those by birth and those he "adopted," like our boys, cultivating their love of music, their sense of fun, and love of adventure.

Like a cell that replicates before it dies, he'd left his mark, and a part of Anthony will be carried on in each of them.

He was ready. Even if we weren't.

Somehow, as I have come to realize this, I haven't cried for Anthony anymore. In its own way, his life was perfect, and he lived it fully.

I may cry again, selfishly, missing his laugh and his company and the ease of his friendship. But when I catch myself feeling like something is missing, I have to remind myself. Anthony lived a perfect life, and in its own way, its end was perfect, too.

## The Art of Grieving

Anthony's death drew our family together in a way only death can. We drew into each other, resting in the sense of family that sustained us during what felt like unutterable pain.

The boys took Anthony's death hard.

Little Michael was standing in the doorway of the office when we first got the call, and he crumpled on the floor as he listened; when we hung up, he crawled over and sat in my lap, his wet face buried in my shoulder.

Dereck and Matthew reacted the same way when we picked them up from day camp.

Daddy Michael was inconsolable—shaky, eyes swollen with tears, he kept repeating over and over, "I can't believe it. I can't believe it."

There was something grace-filled about the boys' and Michael's tears, the purity of their grief, the complete sense of loss and love for a man they loved beyond measure.

Even Mo, who'd loved Anthony, too, knew something was wrong, and she paced between us, putting her paw on our legs, the worry furrowed into the skin around her sad brown eyes.

As for me, it seemed like the air had been sucked out of my own lungs. It was a struggle to breathe; the weight of a thousand stones crushed my chest.

His brothers asked us to help organize the funeral, and they asked me if I would give the eulogy. I wrote the obituary they submitted to the *Los Angeles Times* and interviewed the musicians we hired to play at the funeral and the celebration party after. I threw myself into the tasks, grateful that my mind had to focus on words and plans and activity, instead of being free to wander in the shadows.

It was only after the night I dreamt of how Anthony chose to die that I really began to feel that enormous, gaping grief that had ripped open my heart. How would the enormous hole Anthony left in our family and in my own life ever be filled?

The first time I met Anthony, he stuck his hand out to shake mine, and I remember thinking, "This guy's got the biggest hands I've ever seen." I made some remark about it, and he flashed his big, wide grin and said, "Big hands, big heart."

When we met, I had just started going out with Michael, and there was no way Anthony would allow Michael to have an important relationship without his approval. So we invited him to dinner. I was scared stiff.

I can't remember what I cooked that night, but I'll never forget Anthony sitting at the opposite end of the table, his piercing eyes fixed on me, grilling me with question after question.

When he was done, and I was a lifeless blob crumpled in my chair, he looked over at Michael and said, "Well, I think he's okay."

And then he did the most extraordinary thing. He told us to settle down on the couch, and he went to the piano upstairs in the loft.

He'd already picked out songs he thought I would like, and he sat at the piano to serenade us. Like everything Anthony did, the singing and the playing and the choice of songs were pitch perfect.

From that day on, Anthony became a big and important part of my life.

When Michael and I had our commitment ceremony, we asked Anthony to give the toast. He said no at least ten times because he was extremely shy about speaking in public.

Finally, he relented and said yes—because he didn't trust anyone else to do the toast the way he thought it should be done.

Just before the ceremony started, when I was so nervous I thought I was going to throw up, I looked over at Anthony. He was sweating more than I was. He gave me the cocked eyebrow and whispered, "You know I'd only do this for you."

Anthony's toast was perfect. He spoke from his big heart, and there wasn't a dry eye in the house.

When Michael and I first began the adoption process, going through classes and training and endless home inspections, Anthony was right there with us; he wanted us to be parents, and he wanted to make sure we knew it. He walked with us on the journey, steadying, calming, focused, helping us keep our eye on the end goal, no matter how frustrating the latest bit of bureaucracy happened to be.

From the moment Anthony met the boys, he was like Auntie Mame. He fell in love with them and they with him. The night the boys came home for the first time, Anthony was there, ready to welcome them with his big, booming voice and big hugs.

After our first dinner around the table, we all walked down to the Hollywood Bowl to see k.d. lang and Rufus Wainwright. Matthew sat in Anthony's lap during much of the concert. Anthony, who loved k.d., crooned along into his ear.

He was always ready to introduce them to new things—everything from his favorite book, *Walter the Farting Dog*, to his famously disgusting avocado cheesecake, to all the life lessons he thought important.

He made it his goal to teach our boys table manners. He ate dinner with us at least once a week, every week. He'd always say, wagging his big fingers at them, "Sit up straight! Elbows off the table! My mother used to bang my elbows on the table if she ever saw them there! You're lucky I don't do that to you!"

When Anthony was around, they listened: Napkins in their laps. Knife and fork held properly. Ramrod straight posture. All done with rolling eyes and sighs. But it was with respect because they loved Uncle Anthony and knew that if he thought table manners were important, they must be.

Matthew's second grade class had a guest reader each week; all the parents were asked to come to read a story or invite someone who could entertain the class. It was our turn around Halloween, and I asked Anthony if he'd be willing to read. He came to class and read a story about friendly vampires and werewolves and goblins that all learned to live together, and he made up special voices for each character.

The kids were entranced. Astonished that her usually unruly class was silent and completely enraptured by Anthony's story, Ms. Carrie, Matthew's teacher, whispered, "He's amazing!" And so he was.

Afterward, Matthew's cache in class grew. "That's *my* Uncle Anthony," he gloated all week.

When Dereck had to do his California mission project, Uncle Anthony told him to pick the St. Anthony of Padua Mission because he was named after that saint.

Anthony decided it was *his* mission to help Dereck build the replica of the mission. Anthony treated that mission project with the same intensity, creativity, and thoroughness he brought to everything he did. Every night for a week, they labored on it together.

When they were done, it was an architectural wonder: hand-painted tiles, a carefully sculpted tower with a working bell, grazing cattle, and perfect miniature Romanesque arches. It was more a museum piece than a fourth-grade project.

Dereck got an A. And Uncle Anthony got to take the mission home, where he proudly displayed it in a place of prominence—on a shelf in his garage.

Before the funeral, Dereck wrote him a letter in his journal. One of the sentences he wrote made me cry: *Uncle Anthony, I love you and I will be thinking of you in heaven.... But who will help me when I have a project and need your help?*

It's been weeks since Anthony's death, and I keep asking myself the same thing. The phone rings, and I expect it to be him. When I start to set that extra place at the table, I have to remind myself he's not here to share a meal with us. I can't even walk onto our deck without thinking, "Who's going to chastise me for not taking care of the roses?"

When I dreamt of how Anthony took his life, I knew he wanted me to know not only the method he chose but also that he was still present with me.

I cling to that, even as I feel a pain so great I sometimes don't know how to breathe. Somehow, someway, Anthony is still here.

Trying to write something for Anthony's eulogy, I read that when Yoko Ono was asked how she could bear being without John Lennon because they had spent 90 percent of their time together, she said, "Now we spend 100 percent of our time together."

Is it true we each carry with us the indelible imprint of those we love?

I'm not quite sure. But I do know that I feel a big, Anthony-sized handprint on my heart.

Which is exactly as he would like it.

# Getting Older

"God, do we look middle-aged!"

Michael's scanning some pictures of us that had been taken at his cousin's wedding this summer.

I look over his shoulder at the images on his screen. "We don't look that bad!"

"Yeah. But look at us compared to all the thirty-year-olds at the wedding. We look ancient."

Since Anthony's death, I think we are both more mindful of the fleeting nature of life. And we've reached that awful moment when everyone we know suddenly seems a lot younger than we are. We're on the downward slope of the bell curve, there's no two ways about it.

I don't have the faintest clue when it happened. You go merrily along through life until one day it hits you: everyone else is a kid.

In that instant, time is no longer measured in hours or seconds, but in that slow, steady swing of the Grim Reaper's scythe, whistling ever louder in your ear.

Once you're attuned to the inevitable, you hear its sound everywhere.

It's the voice of the young attendant at the counter at the gym who automatically calls you "sir."

It's the voice of your doctor, who looks more tired than you do, when he looks at you undressed and says, "Are you still working out?"

It's the voice in your own head, as you catch yourself standing in the mirror, pulling up both sides of your face, telling yourself just how much better you'd look with a tighter jaw line.

And it's the voices of your children, their boundless energy and their perfect, unlined skin. If nothing else reminds us of the inevitability of aging, the contrast between their puppy-like enthusiasm and our own world weariness will.

Friends told us having kids would keep us young. All it has done is remind us of how tired we are. Chasing after kids, trying to keep up with them, orchestrating play dates, meals, homework, summer projects, and ways for them to earn an allowance make for the most demanding full-time job in the world. It's exhausting.

We live in a state of perpetual bleariness, always on the point of nodding off for a nap. Adrenalin is the only thing that keeps us going. That kind of steady pounding shows up on your face in no time.

I try to remind myself I'm just too busy to worry about looking like an old fart, but it would be like telling a hypochondriac that the brain cancer he's certain he has is nothing more than a Sunday morning hangover.

It might be true, but that's not the point.

The sad thing is, I can fuss and fret inside my head all day long, but I'm too tired to do anything about it. I don't have the energy I had at thirty-five—or at forty, for that matter. By bedtime, I've worked so hard I'm too tired to wash my face, let alone squirt some miracle cream on it that will regenerate my skin while I sleep.

After a near half-century of hard use, I've earned those lines and crinkles and skin tags. They are proud emblems of the wisdom and gravitas that comes with age.

Or so they tell me.

True wisdom wouldn't worry about how threadbare my face and body look, but about the condition of my soul. Like many of my other middle-aged friends, I'm very clear on the concept that we are spiritual beings having a human experience and not the other way around. But I am a vain creature, and I want this human experience to look damn good.

Sure, I'm spiritual, but I still find the choice between shopping and meditation a hard one. I'll haul my butt to the gym long before I'll take the time to sit still and worship. So I know this is a peculiar life lesson for me. The pull of the flesh is strong. And while I wouldn't turn away the wisdom of age, I'm not sure I want it if comes in a wrinkled, withered package.

Christian theologians seem to have some of the same worries as me, and I find that perversely comforting. John Stott, the elder statesman of English theology who is now the poster boy (even though he is in his dotage) for politically active American Christians, notes the natural law that says all bodies will decay was turned upside down by the crucifixion and resurrection of Christ.

It's a cause for great hope for Stott. Even his old body will see a physical regeneration as well as a spiritual one when his Messiah returns. He learned his lesson at the knee of his own teacher, an even older Martyn Lloyd-Jones, who preached that all believers would live in their bodies on a renewed and regenerated earth.

It's sort of nice to know that leading Christian minds worry about the same things I do: what I am going to look like in the afterlife.

Michael claimed not to care too much, until he ran into an old friend at the gym. When he and Dino were in their twenties, they looked similar enough to be brothers, and people often confused them for each other. At forty-eight, Dino has grown into a buff, muscular guy with arms of steel and an unlined, carefree face, the result of living with his mother his entire life.

Seeing him made Michael blanch. "We used to be on par, but I had the bigger muscles. Now I'm carrying thirty extra pounds, and he's got a six-pack." Along with his chronically aching back and chronic worries about the kids, it's one more thing to keep him awake at night.

Which is exactly what we don't need. If anything can slow the inevitable tide, it is sleep. And in our room, it is in short supply. Not from unwarranted hanky-panky, mind you, but from snoring dogs, restless children, and the unreleased accumulation of pressure upon pressure throughout the day that makes sleep more like the sputtering of a slow-release valve than rest.

Our seventeen-year-old daschund, Dart, likes to spend her days sleeping and squinting in the sun. She rouses herself only for food and for a quick trot to some yet-unmarked place on the carpet where she can do her business. She's deaf and nearly blind, and generally irritable and crabby as only an old person can be.

The only thing that really gets her excited anymore is the thought I might drop some morsel from my dinner plate in her direction; she'll jump like a puppy for a piece of chicken. That jump, straining her tired little legs, is an instinct built into her cell memory, the last vestiges of a dog that was quite the hooligan in her day.

I'd give her the chicken even if she didn't jump, but as long as she can do it, I'm happy. It's a reminder of the puppy I once knew, buried somewhere in that tired, fragile little body.

As painful as the thought of aging may be, I hope I turn out like Dart—a little slower, just slightly senile, but still able to rouse myself for the things that bring me pleasure. She doesn't care that her gorgeous ginger fur has gone gray and that her sharp little teeth are brown and spotted.

She doesn't even mind that she has to be carried in a pouch over my shoulder whenever we go for a walk. Her grizzled head poking out of the bag, she squints into the sun and sighs deeply, sniffing at all the scents and odors along the way.

She's just happy to be along for the ride.

And as I scratch her vacant little head, mindful we may not have her too much longer, so am I.

## Fathers and Sons

"Was President Nixon like Hitler?"

We're in the car, driving home from a week in Northern California, and my niece Lindsey, who is with us, uses the time to finish her summer reading assignments for school. She's reading a novel about Vietnam vets and their struggle to return to their old lives. Her mind is sharp and subtle, and she asks lots of questions.

I love the chance to engage her curiosity. Before I can answer, Little Michael, sitting next to her, pops in with his own perspective.

"Hitler was a communist," he shouts out, giggling.

"No, Michael, Hitler wasn't a Communist," I respond.

"Yes he was! Hitler was a Communist, Hitler was a Communist!" He doesn't want to hear serious conversation, and he's intent on being disruptive.

"Michael, you don't know what you're talking about."

He likes that he's gotten under my skin. "Yes I do! Hitler was a Communist!"

Lindsey snorts next to him, making it clear what she thinks about his assessment.

After a week crammed in the car together, I'm not far behind her. "Michael, that's idiotic. I know you know better. You studied World War II last year."

His face suddenly falls. "You called me an idiot."

"I didn't call you an idiot, Michael. I said that was an idiotic statement. There's a big difference. Use the brain God gave you."

But that subtlety is lost on him, and he turns away, lip quivering.

He feels bad, and suddenly, so do I. I could fill a book with all the ways he's been irritating and juvenile this week, pouting, bullying his brothers, and interrupting any conversation that is remotely serious. He turned fifteen two weeks ago, but he acts like he's five.

I know something is going on with him, but the outbursts and disruption have been so constant, I've gotten to the point where I just lash out to shut him down every time he starts.

It's not until we get home that I get the first real clue about what's really bothering him.

Grabbing dinner around the kitchen counter, Michael announces he wants to be a camp counselor again at his old school next summer, like he did last summer. He'd passed on the opportunity after his eighth-grade graduation, claiming he was tired and needed to rest so he'd be ready for high school.

He'd refused to even do extra chores to earn money to hang out with his friends— until midway through the summer when I'd had enough and told him the well had run dry. He'd need to earn spending money if he wanted to do anything social from that point on.

"You're probably going to want a real job, Michael," I shoot back. "You like to go to movies and lunch and to Universal, and you're going to need to make some money to afford it."

There's just a glimmer of vulnerability when he looks over at me and shakes his head. "No. I want to be at camp."

Even then, it doesn't it hit me. My frustration with his behavior has blinded me to what he's feeling. Frustrated and angry, I go to bed asking for guidance, wanting to figure out why he's behaving like such a jerk.

In the morning, it comes. Michael's afraid.

He starts high school in two days. He's afraid of growing up, of things changing faster than he can keep up with. He's afraid of being responsible for new knowledge, for new ways of looking at the world, and for new adult behavior. He wants to stay where it's safe and comfortable and he knows the lay of the land.

Of course.

My hard-ass comments and constant talk of responsibility and growing up didn't do anything to address symptoms, let alone the root cause of his acting out. It had just made him feel worse. And what's even harder is the recognition that I'm not just guilty of failing to understand his fear.

As a parent, you know you're supposed to love your child exactly as he is. I have no doubt I love him deeply, fully, and truly. I just don't like him very much right now, and it shows. I've let what I see as his offensive behavior blind me to the scared little boy underneath.

I vow to be more compassionate, but when Michael balls up his new shirts in the corner of his filthy bedroom, I yell again.

But even as I yell, I realize this isn't the way to help him, not the way to help myself. So when I'm done, embarrassed and agitated as I am, I take a deep breath and try to explain why balling up brand-new clothes is not a good thing.

Seeing my effort, Little Michael is sheepish and apologizes, and I do, too. The path to adulthood isn't easy, but maybe we can navigate it together.

# Stepford Children

"You've got the biggest heart in the world," my old boss exclaims when we chat on the phone, catching up. It's been more than two years since we saw each other last.

"Oh, no, oh, no," I respond, and I mean it.

I'm not trusting the condition of my heart these days. It feels like a very dark place, full of frustration and fear, a far cry from the clean and open space that once welcomed children like we were all going on a picnic in the park.

The constant bickering and carpools and chasing after messes and dealing with smart mouths and snappy attitudes have cast a long, dark shadow. My heart feels like it is shrinking from a lack of light.

We met some friends during our family vacation before school, and they had just sent their second child off to college. "How's it been having the house to yourselves?" we asked.

Gary suddenly beamed. "I don't drink anymore! I never realized how much I was drinking just to deal with the stress of having them around."

A year ago I would have been horrified. Today, I'm ready to raise a glass in his honor.

If you're not careful, your children can beat you down.

Most of us who become parents do so with the best intentions. We want to bring a child into the world and lovingly raise it, teaching it all we know, imparting our values and beliefs to a new and eager generation. We tell ourselves we will never make the same mistakes our own parents did, and that our child will be like Mary Poppins, practically perfect in every way.

As long as they go along with that plan, everything is fine. But the minute they figure out they've got their own minds and their own wills and begin the inevitable assertion of their own personalities, the stage is set for World War III.

Before long, we wonder if we can exchange the little darlings for some Stepford children.

Yesterday, I took Michael and Dereck for haircuts, which is always an epic battle about control. They both like to wear their hair long, hanging far below their eyes and over their collars. When it gets long enough to get caught in their food when they try to chew, I warn them the appointment is coming. They're consuming enough outside protein and don't need to eat their own.

Every time, they whine for days; every time, I have to signal their barber Rod behind their backs about how much to chop off. And every time, they get emotional about the shiny, well-shaped and still-too-long coif they have when they are through.

Michael says his head is too small and refuses to believe his thick, unkempt mass makes it look even smaller. His nostrils turn pink and his eyes water every time he gets up from the barber's chair, convinced he's now a pinhead. He flashes darts of guilt in my direction, not daring to say, "How could you do this to me?"

Dereck just gets mad because he doesn't have the final say about how much is cut off. Furious red blotches break out on his neck and ears, and he won't look at me or Rod or anyone else for at least an hour. Instead, he'll walk around tugging at the hair that still hangs into his eyes, as if he can make it even longer by sheer force of will.

They don't get that their newly shaped heads are actually a compromise; if it were all up to me, they'd have crew cuts. Given their druthers, their hair would eventually trail behind them, collecting even more dust and dirt than it already does.

Still, they can't escape the fact they look better and they *smell* better. With handsome young faces visible for all the world to see, the universe has a wonderful way of affirming them. Within a few hours of their haircuts, someone invariably compliments them. They glower, but it sinks in. Maybe a well-trimmed head *is* better than what they had before.

No matter how secretly pleased they might be, it takes them a long time to release their resentment. In their eyes, I've forced them to do something they don't want to do.

Which is why being a parent can be such a lonely, dark place. We have the best intentions for our children, we are motivated to act out of love, and we are often met with a resistance fiercer than anything in today's partisan politics.

If that's not tough love, I don't know what is.

And besides, engaging our children is like looking into a mirror of our own souls. If I'm honest, I am more like my boys than I care to admit. I prefer to have control even when my choices are not the best. If I had hair, I'd choose greasy split ends over clean, shiny locks if someone tried to force to me wash. Take away my choice, and I'm pissed and ready to rebel.

It's all there, a veritable epicenter of the human condition, this relationship between parent and child. The attitudes, the resistance, the refusal to embrace what is best for us is at the root of every self-destructive impulse, every ill that plagues mankind.

From the moment we can walk, from the moment we can speak, we instinctively rebel. Each of us comes into this world convinced that we know better than anyone what is best for us, and we cling to that delusion even when life's realities prove it false.

Like the affirmation that comes after the haircut we're convinced we don't need, we find that when we give up control, life brings us blessing, not pain.

Raising children becomes the crucible where we learn this lesson again and again.

At breakfast, I share with Matthew that I am struggling with my writing in the same way he struggles with his homework. There are moments when I don't know what to say, which way to go, and everything seems black.

I tell him, "I get upset like you do sometimes, Matthew. I read what I wrote, and it doesn't make sense, and it makes me really frustrated. I want to give up. So I have to stop and ask for help before I can go on."

He scratches my back empathetically. "I know, Daddy John, I know."

He grins, and the darkness lifts. Suddenly, my heart does feel like it is the biggest in the world.

# The Bucolics

The sky outside is grey, unusual in September. It matches my mood, still dark, still sad, on this Saturday morning. It's that rare weekend time when I have a few moments of quiet before everyone else in the house stirs. In the minutes before Matthew comes bounding up the stairs, I sit and stare out the window.

The dogs sleep on the floor around me. Three of the four are on multiple medications, and it gets complicated trying to remember which pill goes with which. This morning, as I stood in a daze at the kitchen counter with the prescription bottles and dishes lined up in a row, waiting for the coffee to brew, I worried that I'd give the wrong pill to the wrong dog.

I operate now in a constant state of overwhelm. I don't delude myself anymore into thinking I can stay one step ahead of the boys; it's enough to just keep up with them. Things that used to drive me crazy—like crumb-filled kitchen drawers or a floor that needs a serious wax—I just try to ignore as best I can. I've learned to carve out work time in the quiet spaces when the kids aren't around, learned to live with fewer and fewer hours of sleep, learned to live with the black circles under my eyes that give me a raccoon-like countenance.

Michael and I have gotten used to having conversations that focus almost entirely on schedules and kids' needs and homework, all of it spoken in verbal shorthand that has sprung up out of necessity. Life is all about addressing the nonstop needs of a big family. But underneath those conversations is a deep strain, a sorrow we each carry that neither can fully express.

We all continue to grieve Anthony.

Anthony was Michael's best friend for more than twenty years, the yin to his yang, the friend who carried him along on adventures and who served, in a funny way, as his memory. Anthony never forgot a face or a conversation, and he would always remind Michael of friends and situations and stories that Michael had long forgotten. At the funeral, Michael turned to me and asked, "Who will remind me about my life?"

I think of that question as Matthew walks into my office, precisely at 6:30 as he always does on Saturday mornings, and climbs into my lap. He tells me what he dreamt last night, and he tries to read the story on my screen. "You're writing, Daddy John?" When I say yes, he snuggles in, content to be a part of the process.

"I'm ready for a break, honey. Are you hungry?" He nods, and we go down to the kitchen. I make him the breakfast he always asks for on Saturday morning. He sits at the counter, engrossed in the Cartoon Network, until I put his plate-sized pancake in front of him, soaked in syrup and butter. He giggles and digs in, and his pleasure makes me smile.

Michael and I got one of our rare nights out last night, stopping at our friend Tony's fortieth birthday party before heading to a school function.

Tony introduced us around as "the guys who adopted these three amazing kids," and we go through an endless round of how lucky they are and how lucky we are. As we said good night, I hugged and kissed Tony. "For me, birthdays are always a time to think about what I really want from life," I told him. "From everything you've been saying, I have a feeling you might want to start a family."

For just a moment, his eyes got misty, and he nodded.

We went on to the school function, hanging with our friends Lisa and Angelina, who each have a son Michael's age. The boys are all entering puberty, and when they are together, they sound like a bunch of squawking birds. Each of them is mortified by their inability to control their voices, and we parents all find it adorable. The puberty stories flew fast and furious. "I kept yelling at Michael to wash his face for two weeks before I realized it was time to buy him a razor," I cracked.

Lisa giggled. "Oh, crap. I thought Dylan was just eating too much chocolate before I came here tonight. Where's the nearest twenty-four-hour drug store?"

A couple of parents we didn't know drifted into our little circle, and we all continued to share stories and laugh. "Do your boys look like you?" one of them asked.

"Oh no," I said. "We adopted them."

They have the standard reaction of almost every parent we meet. "Three boys. That's quite a challenge! How long have you had them?"

"It's only been two years," I answered, "but it feels like forever."

Indeed, our lives have this smooth surface, an easiness that looks effortless to the untrained eye. We have what we have worked for, and it is as rich and wonderful as we knew it would be.

Our friend Jens calls us "The Bucolics," like our lives are a throwback to some pastoral scene in the English countryside. "If I didn't see it, I wouldn't believe people live like you anymore," he says. I know he's paying attention; his wife Emily is due to give birth to their first child in nine weeks, and they asked us to host the baby shower.

"Maybe your kids' energy will rub off on our little one," he says ruefully, with that tiny, stubborn bit of fear no expectant father can shake.

"Are you really sure that's what you want?" I laughingly tell him.

But I feel far from bucolic inside. I can't seem to shake the overwhelming feeling of loss, the deep sense of hopelessness that sits like a stone underneath the smooth surface. It's been months since Anthony took his own life, and the effects of his death are taking its toll on me. Anthony's death has taken the wind out of my sails.

I love making Matthew's breakfast, but there's a part of me that wants to run as far away as I can go. I remind myself over and again that I am not responsible for Anthony's choice, but the nagging voice in my head that blames me for not stepping in runs like a continuous loop.

I worry about our boys, knowing their seeming diffidence to Anthony's death is just a way for them to cope with one more loss. I worry their buried pain makes them vulnerable to the same addiction that took the mother and the uncle they love from their young lives. And I see Michael suffer, his pain so acute he can barely function, and there seems nothing I can say or do that relieves his suffering.

It all feels so overwhelming, I sometimes don't know how to put one foot in front of the other. In a way, having children and a household makes it easier; someone has to cook and feed the dogs and make sure the laundry is done. I tell myself, "Focus on the little tasks, and it will all work itself out."

But when I wake up in the middle of the night, my heart racing, gripped in sadness and a fear I can't begin to describe, I wonder. I feel like I am suffocating, the weight of breakfasts and addictions and suicide pressing down on my heart and lungs.

For the first time, I get a glimmer of why my aunt chose to flee, why my grandmother disappeared for months at a time. Their lives must have felt so unmanageable, it was the only choice they knew to make.

When I sent an editor friend some early drafts of my stories about the boys, she told me point-blank she didn't think they would make a good book. "Adoption stories don't sell," she said. "And besides, there's not enough dramatic tension. Where's the storm and fire?"

I was offended at first, but there was some truth to her feedback. The storm and fire don't come from the kids or the new life we have built. They come from the struggles of everyday life, from loving and loss, from the yearning to make my children and those I care for immune from things that can cause them pain.

I can't protect them, just as I can't protect myself. This is nothing more than a natural cycle in life, part of what gives it meaning, what opens the door to an experience of grace. I think of the Psalmist who wrote, "Weeping may spend the night, but joy comes in the morning."

I have not found that joy yet, but I cling to the hope, knowing that in my sorrow, in the sadness I feel for Anthony and the huge empty space he has left in my life, in Michael's life, and in our children's lives, there is fertile ground for joy to take root and grow.

So I get up in the morning, and I make breakfast for Matthew and focus on those little tasks that occupy my hands and sometimes my mind. I choose to live in trust that somehow, in the soil of our sorrow, roots of joy are growing, even if they have not yet broken the surface. I long for that joy to grow and spread, like one of those mighty banyans, so broad and vast that it looks like an entire forest but is actually a single tree. If joy does come in the morning, I water that soil and hope and wait.

# Even Porn Stars Need Wrapping Paper

When our kids' school sold Sally Foster wrapping paper as a fund-raiser, I wrote an appeal and e-mailed it to all our friends and family. Family immediately said yes, and the friends with kids who know they can count on us for a quid pro quo did the same.

Our friend Gregg never mentioned my e-mail, but I didn't think twice about it. A struggling actor, he's never flush with cash, and he's been forced to dabble in real estate, take demeaning infomercials, and hawk aspirin and car insurance on TV to make ends meet.

No need for him to waste his money on wrapping paper.

Gregg's a sweet guy, very straight, very all-American, and a magnet for high-powered women who like his rugged good looks and affable manner. He fell hard for a financier last year, and when she dumped him, we were his sounding board as he poured out his sorrow.

I see Gregg every morning at the gym, and often during the day whenever the TV is on, shilling some new product. But last night, while I was channel surfing to find something to lull me to sleep, I saw Gregg in a whole new light.

On the premium movie channels, you'll find a lot of silly soft porn intermixed with more conventional films. The soft porn is pretty lame, especially if surgically enhanced women are not your cup of tea. As I click past, I laugh and wonder just who watches it.

But last night, on my way to a *Real Time with Bill Maher* rerun, I stopped short on a Cinemax channel. There was Gregg, coupling with one of those silicone-wonders, his big hands glommed onto breasts that had to be 75 percent fake.

I guess the last State Farm commercial wasn't paying enough residuals.

This morning, Gregg sat down next to me to do sit-ups at the gym. Just as I was about to tease him about his most recent cinematic venture, he said, "Hey, I just got the wrapping paper I ordered for the kids. Not sure what I'll do with it all, but I ordered enough to get the free shipping."

It was on the tip of my tongue to suggest he could come up with a lot of creative uses for it. But I stopped myself and simply thanked him.

"Anything for those boys. When are we going to play catch again?"

"Whenever you've got some time," I replied, and then paused. "Hey, now I see why you don't need a mitt when you play catch."

"Oh yeah?"

"I never realized just how much your hands could hold until I saw you on TV last night."

He looked puzzled for a moment, and then turned beet red. "You saw?"

I nodded.

Sheepish, he said, "I needed the money."

"And you spent some of it on wrapping paper? What a sweet, sweet thing to do, my friend." He laughed, and I laughed. "Okay Gregg, I've got to ask," I said. "What does a fake boob feel like?"

"It's about as real as everything else you saw in that scene."

"Well, that's good to know. I'd hate to think I'm missing out on something."

"It pays the bills, man, it pays the bills."

"And buys the wrapping paper," I laughed again. If only Sally Foster knew.

## A Knife in the Heart

Sometimes your kid is just going to hate you, and there's not a lot you can do about it.

I yelled at Dereck on Friday night for flipping on his skateboard in his room. In some households, that's not a big deal, but in our cramped, noisy space, the thumping and banging not only shakes the floor, it really gets on our nerves.

He's been asked politely, then firmly told not to do it a million times already, but it somehow hasn't sunk in. On Friday, Tracy's son Richard was hanging out, he did it again. And again, and again, until finally, I marched downstairs and took the skateboard away.

Embarrassed in front of his friend, Dereck cried, flinging out all the excuses and justifications he could think of. He was just playing. Some of his friends get to skateboard in their houses, so why shouldn't he? He's just a kid and kids are supposed to have fun.

The steam coming from my ears made me deaf to his pleas.

Finally, when nothing else seemed to work, he decided to pull out the big guns. "You're so mean! I hate you!"

For any parent, that's like a knife in the heart.

Even if I know he doesn't really mean it. Even if he can't even remember he said it the next morning. Words like these have staying power.

My mom used to say the best thing parents can do is to develop a thick skin.

She's probably right. I lay in bed all that night, fretting, alternating between fury and slobbery, self-pitying tears.

We all want our kids to love us unconditionally, to adore us with wide-eyed wonder because we're so darn terrific.

But there's a wicked reality that belies all that wishful thinking.

Again, as my mother used to say, "The apple doesn't fall far from the tree."

Even if that tree's been grafted; adopted boys tend to take on the characteristics, both good and bad, of the dads who took them in.

Which is to say that parenting is an imperfect art, and the children we love are a reflection of that imperfection. So my boys, no matter how much I do my best, are just as prone to making mistakes and being hateful and mean as I am.

I see in Dereck's obstinacy, his willingness to lash out, his hard edge when he's confronted with his own shortcomings, a mirror of the dad who is a like a dog with a bone when he's yelling at his kids.

I've been known to master a mean-spirited turn-of-phrase in my day. It is no wonder my little 'wunderkind' can do the same.

That doesn't take away any of the sting, but it offers a different frame of reference when I think about what I want to encourage in my son.

For a kid to say "I hate you" is a defensive retort, the cry of the maligned. Sure, he may be responsible, even at twelve, for the things that come out of his mouth. But he's operating in a world where his singular point of reference happens to be me.

So the question, all thick or not-so-thick skin aside, is what am I doing to create a dynamic where he feels his only option is to lash out?

That dog with a bone sure knows how to bully when his dander is up. And that's not the best approach if I want to foster loving within my children and in their connection to me.

Parenthood is all about good intentions, and sometimes good intentions can go awry.

We walk a fine line, trying to encourage our kids to make good choices; we try to set parameters that work for them and for everyone in the household; we pay attention, devising little course corrections when there is a need.

We try to love unconditionally, and there's a moment we fail. One blow-up, one loud yell, and we run the risk of unraveling all that careful effort.

It's easy to despair and want to call it a day. But when a kid is looking at you with hungry eyes, longing to know you love them even when they mess up, staying in your anger and hurt just isn't an option.

And when you look in the mirror, and see those same hungry eyes staring back at you, giving up isn't option there, either.

Sometimes your kid is just going to hate you, and there's not a lot you can do about it. Except to love them, and love yourself, as best you can.

## Ciao, Nonna

I reach over and gently rub the top of her head, the pink scalp shiny underneath the shock of white hair. Her eyes, once sharp and hazel like mine, are now dark and dim, and as I rub, she half-closes them, nodding ever so slightly.

Grandma always loved to have her head rubbed, and even now, though she no longer knows who I am, I know she will begin to relax and nod off, just like she did when I was a boy.

Sure enough, her eyes close, and her head turns slightly, resting against the back of her wheelchair. Her mouth falls open and her hands, still strong, unfold in her lap.

I kiss her forehead and walk away, leaving my grandmother in her chair in the nursing home, set in the beautiful rolling hills outside Cleveland. Losing my other grandmother earlier this year stoked a fire within me to visit this grandmother; I was able to make the trip as part of a business trip and take an extra day to visit her.

It was a shock to see her, the first time in two years. She spends her day in her wheelchair now, her white hair that was once dyed jet-black surrounds a face that has lost all its bony angularity.

When I walked up to her, her eyes had looked right through me. "Who you?" she demanded as I bent down next to her chair.

"It's Peep. Your grandson." From the moment I was born, I was called Peep, short for *pepino*, or "little one," in Italian.

"Who?"

I repeated it again.

"Peep? You kidding! Oh, you come to see me." For a moment, she remembers.

I wheeled her near a window, and she stared out as I sit next to her, holding her hand. She looks frail, but flashes of her old strength remain. She squeezes my hand tight, and I remember how she would love to beat me arm wrestling when she was seventy-five, proud that she was still stronger than most men.

I ask her questions, in English and Italian, to see what she remembers. Her memory is scrambled; she answers in English to my Italian and in Italian to my English. She recites the address where she'd lived for fifty years and the names of her sisters and brothers.

But she can't remember her children's names, and as she struggles to recall, her face twists in frustration, angry she's lost the memory of what was most precious to her. Her hands clench and beat the tops of her legs. She knows she is missing something important.

Once she's used to my presence, she turns to me and asks, "You got kids?" Just a couple of years ago, when her mind was just beginning to recede, she'd been captivated by their story.

"Yes, Grandma. Three boys."

Something stirs in her. "Where's their mother?"

"I'm not sure, Grandma."

"*Putana*. What kind of mother could leave their kids." She says it not like a question, but a statement.

At lunch, I feed her a bit of mashed potatoes and gravy, and some ravioli the nurse's aide warmed up from dinner the night before. "Eva likes her pasta," she said.

I had to coax her to eat, this woman who once could eat me under the table. She'd set her jaw and say "No more" after every bite. But I put the spoon with the ravioli under her nose, so she could smell the sauce. Reflexively, she'd open her mouth, saying "M-m-m-m-m" as she chewed.

As I walk away from the nursing home back to my rented car, I know I'll never see her again.

I drive to the airport, filling my mind with work on the flight back to Los Angeles, jumping back into a crazy schedule when I get home.

But this morning, the house is quiet—the kids are in school—and I sit with memories and a sadness so great I don't know what to do. I see myself on that drive to the airport, consciously willing myself to not feel a sense of loss, cutting it off before it overwhelmed me.

Grandma feels no pain, and I don't grieve for that. I grieve for the lifetime of memories, wiped clean and gone forever.

She was the stuff of legend. Born in the mountains of Italy, her earlobes bear the scars where Mussolini's soldiers ripped the gold hoops from her ears as a child, taking all the gold they could find to pay for his fledgling army. At fifteen, she boarded a boat to come to the United States, worked in factories all her life, and married a man she fought with every day for nearly fifty years.

She woke at 4:30 every morning to do the laundry and clean her house before going to work, clipped her immaculate lawn with shears, and when she nearly died having her third child and her doctor warned her that another delivery would kill her, she told her priest to go fuck himself when he tried to forbid an operation to tie her fallopian tubes. "You're not the boss of me," she said.

She beat a man unconscious when she was nearly eighty when he tried to steal her purse at a bus stop, and until she sold her house at eighty-five, she painted the outside brick and mortar every six months, whether it needed it or not.

She was a force of nature.

And she loved me fiercely, showing me a tenderness the rest of the world never saw. I heard the stories of her life, asking again and again to hear about working in the Chef Boyardee factory or climbing the mountains with the goats. I cherished her stories like jewels, and she rewarded me, taking me back to Italy to see the house and the village where she grew up.

Even after I moved to California, until her memory faded, we talked at least once a week on the phone, and the last thing she would always say was, "Come see me before I die."

"I will. *Promesso*," I'd always say. I promise.

The woman in the wheelchair doesn't know I've tried to keep my promise. She doesn't know I grieve for the memories she's lost, the stories I tell my children that I hope they, too, will remember. I grieve for how quickly ninety-one years on this earth can pass, a short breath from oblivion, how quickly the fierce spark of life is dimmed.

And I grieve for the woman who loved me, who saw in my life all the promise she did not find in her own, who poured her heart and soul into me. How will my children ever know how much her love infused the life I live now, thousands of miles from that little nursing home in the Ohio hills?

## Ghosts

I saw a ghost last night.

I woke from a dream, slowly remembering I was sleeping in a strange room. For the past few nights, we've slept in our friend Richard's guest room, two doors away from our house. My parents are visiting for Thanksgiving, and we've given them our room.

Richard's guest room is small, the double bed facing French doors that open onto a tiny patio. The patio is lit by small twinkle lights; they reflect into the room, not bright enough to overwhelm, but just enough to cast the room in a soft glow.

The ghost was tall, thin, and wearing a muddy brown overcoat. His head was bent, so I couldn't see his face clearly. He stood watch at the end of the bed, looking down at us, still and somber.

I gasped out loud when I saw him and burrowed deep into the covers, hoping he would go away. I peeked out again, and he was still there, not moving.

He didn't seem malevolent, so I blessed him and tried to go back to sleep.

Every few moments, I looked up, and he was still there, never moving, watching as Michael slept and I tried to go back to sleep.

All through the night, I felt unbearable sadness.

We put up our Christmas tree earlier in the evening, the kids dragging out the boxes of ornaments and excitedly loading up the tree.

Matthew found the box containing all the glass fish ornaments our friend Anthony had given us each year for the last few years. "It's Uncle Anthony's fish," he yelled over the din around the tree. Matthew's countenance changed, suddenly no longer merry. He gingerly took them from their wrapping and set them aside on a chair. "We should put these up together," he said, so sad and solemn for an eight-year-old boy.

For a brief moment, his brothers stopped their race to trim the tree, lost in thought. "Good idea, Matthew," his oldest brother agreed. As soon as the lights and the garland and all the other ornaments were on the tree, we all gathered in a semicircle around it, Daddy Michael, the boys, my parents, and me, each holding one of the beautiful ornamental fish.

Michael turned to me. "Daddy John, why don't you say a prayer for Uncle Anthony, since this is our first Christmas without him?"

I found myself choking up, almost unable to speak. "I don't know if I can," I managed to get out.

I looked over at my mom and saw her eyes were wet. She'd only met Anthony once, but she knew how much he meant to all of us. She nodded at me, her way of telling me this was important for the boys.

"Okay," I said, and I closed my eyes. I took a deep breath and said, "Let's pray."

I was silent for a moment, and then I proceeded. "Dear God, thank you for these beautiful ornaments that remind us of Uncle Anthony and how much he loved each of us. Please bless him with you in heaven. And please help us to carry Uncle Anthony's memory in our hearts, just like this tree holds these beautiful fish. We pray in your name. Amen."

Everyone said, "Amen," and gently added Uncle Anthony's fish to the tree.

"It's a beautiful tree," my mom said very quietly as she patted my arm.

After, as my dad napped on the couch, the boys and Grandma played *Sorry!* I watched them, nursing my sadness. Again, I am feeling the weight of Anthony's loss, something that has come over and again since the week he died; once the grief has hold of me, it's nearly impossible to escape.

Daddy Michael cries at odd times, remembering him, and when the boys found a picture of them with Uncle Anthony, taken at a picnic last summer, they made it their screensaver on the family computer. But I'd tried to be stoic, even when the weight of my grief felt so overwhelming I could sink; like my mom, I believe grief should be expressed in private, and so I have held it in.

But not tonight. It took the sight of some kitschy ornamental fish for the dam to finally burst. I had to excuse myself constantly to go into the bathroom to cry. I felt the big chunk that had been torn out of our family and from my heart.

When we walked over to Richard's and climbed into bed, Michael fell asleep almost immediately. I lay awake for a long time, teary, my insides fluttery, until finally, dreams came.

Richard's quipped more than once that his house must be haunted, and strange things have happened since he moved in a year ago. Keys have disappeared and reappeared, doors have suddenly flung open unexpectedly and things moved without explanation. Richard's dog, Sydney, has barked at an empty corner, the fur on her back standing upright.

Although he senses the presence, Richard has never actually seen anything.

So why tonight—and why me?

Perhaps it's my fatigue, the exhaustion of cooking Thanksgiving dinner, of keeping four bored kids occupied over a long holiday weekend. Or perhaps it is because I finally allowed myself to miss Anthony, acknowledging all the ghosts that dwell in my own life.

Whatever the reason, I'm an easy target. There's no barrier to entry.

Our friend Belinda tells us ghosts appear because they are lost and need to find their way. They need for us to help them. She tells me to envision a portal opening in front of the ghost that will allow him to step through, so he can leave the place where he is trapped and get on to where he belongs.

I feel like making a deal with this ghost. I'll do it for him if he'll do it for me. There has to be a sweet other side where fatigue and sorrow have no place.

Anthony's ghost, if it is that, haunts me, as do so many other friends who have suffered and gone on. At times, their memories descend like a shroud, wrapping my heart, diffusing the light, keeping me in a dark place. I look for my portal, and I find none.

But in the dark night there is always a promise of morning. And just like this ghost, who slowly fades as the morning breaks the sky, our ghosts diminish, even if they never leave completely. We can get on with the day, knowing they stand watch, an ever-present shadow that reminds us of all we've loved and lost.

# Epilogue

## As Natural As Breathing

At the end of July 2007, we mark our third anniversary as a family. Apart from mentioning it to friends, there is no fanfare or celebration, just the normal, slightly lazy activity typical to midsummer.

Little Michael and Dereck spend the day at surf camp, learning to ride the mild waves in Santa Monica. Matthew enjoys summer camp at the Schoolhouse, playing and making crafts all day. They are in full vacation mode, fully intent on play. They are boys in summer—they do not want to give any attention to schoolwork or chores or anything that smacks of effort.

Daddy Michael spends the day working out logistics for an upcoming photo shoot, and I put in a full day's work, now at UCLA doing fund-raising.

We come together at the end of the day to have dinner on the deck, appreciating a fine view of the Hollywood hills. From my chair, I watch a gorgeous sunset settling over the dome of the Griffith Observatory and all the homes on the surrounding hillside, Anthony's old house among them. Everything is cast in a pinkish, rosy glow, and I raise my glass of water in that direction, thinking of him again.

The dogs cluster around the table, employing all their tricks to get our attention, waiting for some scrap of food to come their way. Words fly around the table in short bursts, multiple conversations happening at once. We speak in a kind of shorthand, the insular language families develop over time.

Little Michael, almost sixteen, slumps over his dish like he always does, his long, lank hair almost touching his food. Dereck, a determined twelve-year-old, toys with the vegetables on his plate, hoping as he does nearly every night that the act of moving them around will cause them to magically disappear before he has to eat them. And Matthew, still the baby at eight and always the livewire, does karate moves and constantly leaps in his seat, giggling and raucous.

I know without their saying that as we mark our anniversary, the boys remember their birth mom and the life they had before us, but while their memories do not fade, the pull to their life before does not seem as strong.

They bicker over whose turn it is to clean the kitchen and noisily scrape plates and shuffle in to load the dishwasher. It's days like this that make it feel like we've been a family forever. It's easy, it's comfortable, and I revel in it.

Sitting at the table, hearing the noise of clattering dishes and half-aware of the pacing dogs around me, I watch the sunset on the hills, thinking of the last three years.

It has been a long and rich road from our days on the Camino. Three summers ago, I fretted and worried I wouldn't know how to be a father, wouldn't know how to take care of the boys, wouldn't have the faintest clue about what to do.

And somehow, despite all the doubt and second-guessing, the moment the boys arrived, some paternal instinct kicked in. And sometime after, in an undefined moment I still can't place, there was an imperceptible shift. Without fanfare, without a trumpet's blare, I knew, down to my core, I *was* a father.

Fatherhood has become as natural as breathing.